IN HIS SHADOW

Growing Up with Reggie White

JEREMY WHITE

ISBN-10: 1-59670-185-4
ISBN-13: 978-1-59670-185-4

Front cover photo by Barry Cox/Barry Cox Photography
Back cover photo by Valerie Fletcher

Unless otherwise indicated all photos courtesy of Sara and Jeremy White.

Printed in the United States of America

To my mother, Sara, for teaching me optimism
and always believing in me.

Jeremy and his mother,
Sara White

Foreword

I'm humbled that Jeremy White asked me to write a foreword to this book. I know what it's like to lose your father, and I hope that I can come close to honoring Jeremy's dad the way Reggie honored me for so many years, before and after his playing career.

Reggie White's sudden death in December of 2004 shocked everyone associated with the Packers, the NFL, everyone who ever met him, and, really, everyone in this country who never met him. It really shocked me, though, because I had spoken to him just one week before he passed away. He was trying to put together a project with a few NFL players.

Two days before he died, the Packers went into Minnesota and pulled out a win to clinch the division title, so I was on an emotional roller coaster that week. I was honored that Sara, Jeremy and Jecolia asked me to serve as one of Reggie's pallbearers. Then, three days after his funeral, we went into Chicago to play the Bears, and our team gave Reggie his own locker at Soldier Field that morning, with his jersey hanging there and his nameplate at the top. Believe me, I was thinking about him that day, as was everyone.

But I thought about him a lot even before he died. I had the utmost respect for Reggie White as a player. He may have been the best I've ever seen and certainly the best I've ever played with or against.

How good was he? Well, had it not been for Reggie, we don't make it to the Super Bowl in 1996 or 1997. No question, he was paramount to our success. When he signed with the Packers in 1993, he changed the way people viewed Green Bay as a city, and I'm not just talking about people in football—I mean everybody, especially after we won Super Bowl XXXI. He helped the franchise get back to where it had been in the 1960s...at the top.

Our defense was the best in the league during our run, and he made it that way. Teams always feared him because he could turn the course of the game in just one play. I can't even count the number of times he did that for us, it happened so often. I enjoyed watching him play just as much as any fan in the stadium or watching on TV.

With his character and personality, he had a way of attracting people to him even though he was a big man, which can be intimidating to some. That's why he was so successful in fundraising. He did so much, reaching so many people. He even helped me at a charity dinner of mine in Mississippi a couple years before he passed.

It's hard to think that he is gone. On and off the field, he was a great friend of mine and a great friend of my family. We'll all miss him.

Brett Favre

Prologue

There are a few things to know before starting on this epic journey through my life. OK, so maybe it is not so epic, but it is quite a unique journey. I grew up the son of the preacher and the son of a famous football player. I had to share my father with his fans, his parishioners, his community, and God.

I grew up in the shadow of my father everywhere I went. No matter with whom I came into contact, there was that inevitable, "How does it feel being the son of a legend? How does it feel to be the son of a famous superstar? How does it feel to be Reggie White's son?" I tried very hard to stay out from underneath his giant span, and I tried to cut my own path. I was never the one to point out my lineage.

I feel I must indicate that this book is not an array of football stories. This is not because I never went to the games, but I wasn't a diehard fan. I knew my dad sacked people, but I didn't know how many sacks he had a season. I knew that if we kept winning, we'd get to the playoffs and hopefully the Super Bowl; but I didn't know the specifics of how teams made the playoffs. I knew that we had division rivals, but I didn't know how many teams were in the division or why we played them more than once. I viewed my dad as a dad, not a superstar. Getting sacks was what he did for a living. If I were to look up at the stats to enter them here, it would be fake. And I'm not going to pretend to recall, much less be excited about, my dad's everyday work objective when I was five, or seven, or ten years old.

Today, I am much more into football, and I can appreciate my dad's accomplishments completely. I do wish I could have experienced his success, but my favorite team may be surprising. Because football was my dad's job, I am not able to remember how I felt when he set records and had great individual games, no more than my neighbor can remember her feelings when her father set his first broken limb or sewed his first stitches. I was a kid for most of the football years. And like all kids, I just wanted to play. I didn't know about stats; I just knew if Dad was happy with a win, then I wanted him to win.

The names of some people in this book are changed because it isn't in my nature to use my platform to return their offense for the whole world to see. This journey through my childhood and adolescence shows what is important in life: what my dad taught me. And maybe, one may be able to see what it was like to be Reggie White's son. What it was truly like to be *In His Shadow: Growing up with Reggie White.*

1

Sunday, December 26, 2004, 6:30 a.m.

I woke up to my mom nudging me. Did I oversleep? Are we late? What time is it? Man, it's still dark... "Huh?" I hear my own voice say. I try to open my eyes, but they weigh like lead. I just got to bed about 4 a.m. Armella and I were chatting late about love and life.

"Jeremy...Jeremy..." My mom is whispering, but she's breathing heavily. She's gasping in between her words. What? I think, but I don't say it; I just try to roll over. "Jeremy, get up. Jeremy... I think Dad's had a heart attack. Jeremy? Jeremy, get up."

A heart attack. That can't be right.

"I need you to go down the hall and be with Jecolia. But stay outta the way. Don't get in the way of the paramedics. Stay in the guest room. Pray, Jeremy. You and Jecolia need to pray. Pray for your father. Pray for God's will."

"What do you mean? The paramedics are already here? What's going on?" How did I sleep through all that? My feet hit the floor.

"They're shocking him. They're shocking his heart. I tried to do CPR, but I needed help. Go down the hall, but stay outta the way." I turned from my mother, left her in my bedroom to be with my sister. The last thing I heard was Mom praying for God's will to be done. Of course God's will will be done; Dad's gonna be fine.

I found my sister. She was kneeling by the bed in silent prayer. I used the silence to close my eyes. What in the world is going on? I told her, "He's gonna be fine." I don't know if I was trying to convince her or myself. "He's strong. He's the strongest man we know. The man played football for 17 years–man, that's longer than you've been alive."

That was true. In all that time he'd dislocated his shoulders, messed up his knees, tore his hamstring in what should have been a season-ending injury in Green Bay, but God healed him the next week. He'd had cuts and scratches. He'd crashed into thousands of opponents and put his own body through the most vigorous work-outs for so long...he even broke his hand the last year of playing football with the Carolina Panthers. A heart attack was not going to stop this guy. No way.

I went back to bed. About five minutes later my sister came back to ask if I wanted to go to the hospital, like she was asking me if I wanted to go to the mall. I told her no.

Dad's sister, Aunt Christie came into my room, telling me they needed me at the hospital. I woke up as she entered my room like I'd been caught dozing off on the job. She was calm, but peculiar. Boy, she must really be mad I was still asleep. I'm up. I'm up. I have to be the man. They need me for emotional support while Dad is recovering. Only 20 minutes had passed.

Mr. Keith was also with her. As we drove to the hospital in my aunt's truck, I thought about telling her that I made the CDs that she wanted me to make for my dad. On his birthday, December 19, she told me to burn some copies of some oldies that she wanted my dad to have. But now, she was quiet.

There were a lot of friends and family at the hospital. Come on guys, this is my dad we're talking about. A heart attack is not going to stop him. Why are you all so worried? The room was filled more than it should be. What I mistook for concern was truly sorrow. I walked in and saw my mom crying. She looked like all the life was pulled out of her face; she wasn't pale, but ghostlike. I went to her and hugged her. She was droopy. While still holding her I asked, "How is he?"

She looked up through teary, swollen eyes, wiped her nose, and said, "He died."

They tell me I dropped on top of her and started crying. After some friends of the family pulled me up, I fell to my knees, just crying this loud, breathless sob. I remember thinking, "It isn't time for this now." My children are supposed to experience their great big granddad telling the story about separating Brett Favre's shoulder in their first football encounter. And how tough Favre was to stay in the game. And how will they ever know that Granddaddy had such respect from his coaches that they wouldn't cuss him? And his faith. Will I even go back to school next semester? What's going to happen now? I slid into a corner of the room, aware of the growing number of people, folded into myself, and just kept crying. I remember one of the ladies who worked in the condolence room, telling me to stay calm because she didn't want me to hyperventilate. I wiped my eyes. After that I heard someone say, "Did you hear about his dream?"

Oh, wow. His dream.

Just yesterday, Christmas night, we went to the movies like every Christmas night, since there was nothing else to do. We hadn't celebrated Christmas for real in about four years. My sister, who worked at the theater, had finished a shift and was waiting for us. On the way to see *Fat Albert* my dad told my mom and me about a dream he had two nights ago. He said, "I was in the Middle East looking for a treasure. And I came to this building with the treasure in it. Underneath the treasure were inscriptions in Ancient Hebrew letters. I didn't know how to pronounce one word spelled with a Pey, a Dalet, and a Hey. And next in Hebrew it read, 'In Yahovah's name [Yahovah is Hebrew name of God].' After a little bit, the Hey changed to a Yod. So what I saw was 'Pey, Dalet, Hey, and Pey, Dalet, Yod, In Yahovah's name.' I remembered the dream so vividly that I went downstairs when I woke up to check what the Hebrew words meant. Both words that I only could recognize the letters both meant the same thing: redeemed. So what I was looking at was 'Redeemed in Yahovah's name.' Isn't that something?" I couldn't see his face, but I could hear the awe in his voice.

But I remember thinking, "Come on, Dad, you study Hebrew eight hours a day [no exaggeration]. You are bound to have a Hebrew dream." He looked at us, trying to tell us something with his face.

After the movie, Dad was unusually quiet; he didn't talk about the Bible or what he had learned in Hebrew. The only conversation he was interested in was how Bill Cosby gave credit to the original Cosby kids. Respect had been so important to Dad, and he always felt like young people didn't give enough to their elders. Although I was better able to talk to him since we settled our differences when I was a junior in high school, he wasn't responding to my random attempts at conversation. We drove home in silence.

Sitting in that hospital room that day, I interpreted the dream. My dad found the treasure he was looking for, and he was indeed "Redeemed in Yahovah's name." He knew he was all right with God; and then I knew he was all right: my dad was with God. If I had had the time to process that he had passed, it wasn't as if I would have doubted his soul's path; but a dream that he is redeemed two nights earlier is some good confirmation.

I cried big tears with my sister because she had been struggling with my dad, much like I had been just two years ago. I completely understood that unspoken resentment she was feeling; but now, she would not be able to work through it with him. I felt so bad for her, because I knew the guilt she was feeling, but I know Dad understood her conflict.

The doctor asked if we wanted to go in to see him. Mr. Keith came with my mom, Aunt Christie, my sister, and me to the room where they had Dad's body. Mr Keith told us that because we had lost such a good man, the earth would mourn, and there would be earthquakes because of this. He started to pray, to thank God that Reggie was such a good father and leader for our family. I reached for my dad's hand and was surprised it was cold. I wasn't expecting that. I couldn't believe what I was seeing. We were just starting to get close and share that father-son bond. He was lying there on the stretcher with a tube down his throat, but he had just looked asleep. But he was so cold. At that moment I realized that wasn't my father. Dad was no longer in that body. God had him, and I had to remind myself that he was truly redeemed.

But I wondered how in the world I was going to tell everyone about this.

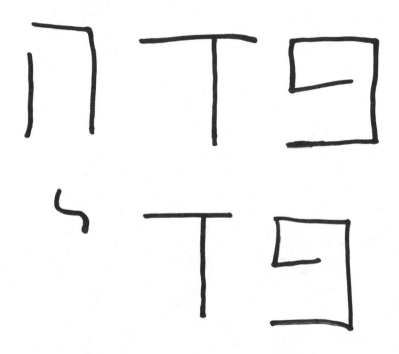

Illustration by Jeremy White

2

Of course when your father is Reggie White, the Minister of Defense, record holder of NFL sacks, you're going to need help telling everyone he died. The media actually assisted my family in a great chore. Mr. Keith Johnson, the former chaplain for the Minnesota Vikings, alerted long-time friend, retired NFL player and current commentator, Cris Carter, to Dad's passing. Cris got permission from Mom and released the death notice on ESPN within hours. And that was that.

Since it was football season, both the pros and the college teams were in full force on December 26; and millions of fans all over the country knew in an instant. Seeing Dad's face with the headline "Reggie White: 1961-2004" was the first step in making it all real. The media saved our family from having to make all those dreaded phone calls to hundreds of people. We didn't have to endure six months of "I just heard." When your dad's Reggie White, the news comes in one quick blast. The healing can begin almost immediately. I didn't have to go back to school and explain my sadness because my dad had died over winter break, and have to hear people say over and over, "Oh." That awkward, what-do-I-say-now "Oh."

Before the broadcast, I had about two hours alone. The first person I called was my friend, Adrienne Zeiler, back in Ohio. I stepped outside the hospital for some privacy. She didn't pick up, so I called Cherie Grant.

"Hey, Cherie, I need you to come to the house. Can you come over right now?" I worked for my voice not to give away any clues. Besides, what would I say? She didn't ask any questions. Her boyfriend drove her 20 minutes just to see why I urged her to come over.

Apparently, Michael Dean Perry offered to drive me home. When we arrived—I don't remember the ride—my across-the-street neighbor came out to offer his assistance. I could hear myself saying, "I'm OK. I'm fine," and I could see my hands out in front of me as a barrier between us. I'm fine; I'm OK. I sounded defensive, like everyone was overreacting. I was on autopilot. Michael Dean Perry walked in the front door with me but then left. I'm sure he said kind words, but I don't remember. I watched him close the front door, get into his car, and drive down the street.

Then the dam burst. I cried in the foyer. The echo resounded the physical pain I was trying to purge. I cried in his trophy room when I saw his caricature statue standing tall in the center. For a moment, I was surprised that figure was still there. I cried in his office as I sat in his chair. On his desk were yesterday's Biblical notes he had meticulously written and a reprinted version of the Dead Sea Scrolls. I scanned the photograph of us in Dad's prized Bel Air when I was four. I cried in my room, and I cried on the way to all of these places. I cried until I didn't have any tears left, and then I cried some more.

I decided I would watch television. That thought ended as quickly as it began because Dad's telephone line rang. I looked at it and hesitated, not certain what to say to the person on the other end. I picked it up, not knowing who could be calling from America's northeast at this time.

"Hello, may I speak with Sara, please?"

"She's not here right now. Can I take a message?" I was careful to show no emotion.

"Is this her son?"

"Yes." Quick syllable.

"Jeremy, this is Andrea Kramer from ESPN. Is everything all right at home? Should I be offering my condolences?"

"I'm...I'm sorry I can't talk right now."

"Jeremy, if..." I heard no more. I hung up the telephone. I couldn't talk to her. I didn't know who she was and I didn't remember meeting her. I couldn't give her any information, because I didn't want to tell the first reporter who called the house that my father had died. I didn't want them to have the "big story." Not at my dad's expense.

Another call on my dad's line again. This time it was from Fox Sports.

"Jeremy, hey, man. James Brown. Hey, can you tell me what's going on, man? The people at the studio are up in arms about something. Is everything OK?"

"James...James, my daddy died." He was the first person I had told. It was the first time I said aloud that Dad had died. The sound resonated in Dad's office, in my brain.

"Oh...aww...oh no, no..." The next part would be said behind tears. "Jeremy, what's your mom's number?" I told him, and he said, "OK, I'm going to call her. I am so sorry about this."

After Mom talked to James Brown, Mr. Keith said not to answer the telephone; he would get someone to handle the phone. But while I was alone in the library, Leonard Wheeler, who would go on to give the greeting at Dad's funeral, called (I had gone in there to log on to my Instant Messenger so my friends could leave me messages. It wouldn't be long now.). I could tell by the caller ID, and I didn't want him to find out through the media. I picked up.

"Hey, Jeremy, what's going on? Your dad called me last night, I was calling him back, is he around?"

"Leonard, I'm sorry I have to tell you this, but he died, man...he's dead."

"Hey, man, Jeremy, you don't need to be playin' like that."

"Leonard, I'm not playing, I swear. He died this morning."

He just paused and said, "Are you serious? . . .man…oh man…." He asked for Mom's number. I don't remember hanging up the telephone; and the people started coming in. Food trays arrived. It was beginning.

At last, Cherie arrived with her boyfriend. I heard her ring the doorbell, and I ran for the head of the stairs. Her boyfriend, Leon, stayed by the front door with Rod Barnes, while she came upstairs, saying, "What's wrong, J?"

"Cherie, my daddy died." I whispered, thinking somehow if I didn't say it, it couldn't be true. My high-school best friend stood slack jawed.

Before long, Joe Pierre, one of my best friends, was calling from Green Bay to say he was going to get down here as fast as he could. I was thinking practically about how much money it would cost for him to get a plane ticket this soon. I told him he really didn't have to come down. He refused to let me talk him out of it (The blessing of the whole situation was that Joe and his family were spared the expense because a friend of ours from Green Bay who flew private planes brought several of our friends for free). The only thing he said was, "Did you hear about the tsunami this morning?" I hadn't heard any news. Nothing else was going on in my world today.

He told me about how thousands of people had died in a tsunami off Sri Lanka that morning. And I thought back to what Mr. Keith said: "There are going to be earthquakes." None of us had seen the television. Mr. Keith was not minimizing the death of over 220,000 people just to make a comforting remark to my family. But for the next week the two top stories on the news were my father's death and the Asian tsunami that occurred seven minutes later.

The day of my dad's death, my mom came up with an idea that demonstrated the clearest thinking. My dad's trophy room held his defensive-player-of-the-year awards, his game balls, the autographed helmets he swapped with other Pro Bowl football players at the Pro Bowl each year he went, 13 years running. And he had all of his jerseys encased in glass. He had his Tennessee Vols jersey, his Memphis Showboats jersey, a Philadelphia Eagles jersey, a Green Bay Packers retired jersey, and all of the Pro Bowl jerseys he had ever worn. During this time many people that we either didn't know that well or hadn't seen in years were coming into our house. For security reasons, in fear of someone having a hidden agenda, my mom asked all of our football friends in the area like Anthony Pleasant, Leonard Wheeler, and Michael Dean Perry if they would help to move the items that might be snuck out of the house into the weight room to be locked up. They started immediately, that same day; and by the next morning, everything was taken out of the trophy room except the jerseys; because no one was walking out with a giant framed jersey.

That week so many people would arrive and everyone who knew about Dad's dream was telling it to one another. It was comforting to them to realize the significance of the dream and what it meant for my dad. Some didn't know how in-depth he was studying Hebrew and how he had picked apart so much of the Bible just to get the clearest understanding of what God wanted him to do. People learned that he no longer went to church because he was studying for himself or had people, like Nehemia Gordon to come and teach him the Hebrew language from an Old Testament perspective.

Friends from everywhere I had lived were meeting one another, which I only thought may happen at my future wedding. It was a reunion for me. All day long, all week long, I was assuring people I was at peace because I knew my dad was ready to go. He had learned so much about God, and he would have kept learning literally until the day he died. My mom agreed. He gave me the reinforcement to live on, to be a man of God, and to make my own decisions.

That week I got different perspectives on what I needed to do now, from being the man to not trying to be Superman, but I came to the conclusion that I would live the way my dad wanted me to live. If I had died instead of him, I wouldn't want him to mope around all day; I would want him to continue doing the things he loved and being the person he was supposed to be. That's what I decided I was going to do.

I needed a moment to myself; I felt the words coming. I went to my room and wrote:

#1 Dad

You were there for me in a different way,
More than words could ever say.
I didn't understand at first,
But every time still another Bible verse—
I cried over all the hard times
And the things that couldn't be mine.
I wondered if there was any chance
Of taking back the years that seem like a glance.
I felt dejected, I feel strange;
I'm not rejected, and I'm not deranged.
I love you and realized this a while back;
Even after the fact
That you had me doing circles like a lost person's map.
I really am going to miss you—
Times will come when I'll want to kiss you.
I'm so glad every night I told u I loved u,
And up until I was 14
Gave you a kiss on the cheek.
No matter how much you put me through,
You had our best interests at heart, not for u;
But for us, your greatest treasures in life.
Next to what? To Yehovah bringing eternal life.
I'm sorry but yet I'm not, because I know
That you are in a better place. That is why
I am at peace, I am feeling sad,
But I want you to know...and I truly mean it with all my heart:
You were the world's greatest!
Rest In Peace, My Father;
And now God guide me farther.

Ironically, during the week of my father's death there were a lot of fun times. I get critical reactions when I say that. How in the world was I able to enjoy myself when my father had just died at 43 years old? I always tell them that it was a reunion of everyone I knew, even though a death brought us all together. We shared stories, we laughed, and we cried.

Late one night during the week right before the funeral, Aunt Maria and Mrs. Bonita Pulido, a family friend since I was 11, each took an Ambien to help them sleep because they were hit pretty hard, as we all were, with the passing of my father. They were both sitting in the kitchen talking when Mrs. Bonita put a potato chip up to her mouth, but it fell from her lips. My Aunt Maria felt the tablet taking effect, and she got out of the chair and said, "Whoa, the floor just jumped at me." These two very proper women looked high.

Also, I asked my mom how much she paid for the casket, because while I knew caskets were costly, an extra-large casket for an extra-large person had to be an expense. Mom was very proud that she got a bargain on it. For certain, if there were coupons for caskets, my mom would have had it. She was always frugal; just because she is well off doesn't mean she would waste "free money," she taught us. She will clip a coupon that saves a quarter if she can.

My mom and I needed those laughs. The only bad part was that Dad wasn't there to tell stories with us. Everything else was how it normally was times ten, because I had all my friends and family with me.

Two days before the funeral 6,000 people flocked to my dad's public viewing. I believe if this viewing had been in Green Bay, Knoxville, or Philadelphia, practically the entire city would have come out to view him. I didn't want to see my dad's body three times. I had already seen his body at the hospital; and when I saw him in the casket, it should be at the funeral and not a moment sooner. I didn't go to the public viewing.

But when Aunt Maria got back with a few other family members and friends, she had quite a story to tell. There was a lady who arrived at the viewing about an hour early and slipped into the bathroom. The lady didn't come out for nearly an hour, and the people running the event found out she was trying to get a jump start on the line that would form to see my father's body. This just goes to show that even after my dad died, there were still fans out there who would do anything to see him.

When I actually found out what killed my father, I was surprised. It was odd because what killed him only happened in .001 percent of the people with his condition. He had sleep apnea, yes. But that isn't solely what killed him. He had sarcoidosis, yes, but that's not what killed him either. The sleep apnea caused him to lose the much needed oxygen during a sarcoidosis attack on his heart. My doctor, who was also his doctor, said that for those two things to occur at the same time was undetectable and was extremely rare. He had traded his eight-hour days of working out for eight-hour days of studying God's Word. He wasn't in his physical prime, but he was ready.

The funeral was on Thursday, December 30, 2004. And surprisingly, it was crunk. It was literally a celebration. I whispered behind tears into my dad's ear my promise to take care of Mom and Jecolia. My sister and I tucked Dad's prayer shawl into the casket with him. Later, I found out Jecolia told my dad, "Jeff Mandel called, and he said he loves you." I had to smile because we were always delivering phone messages to my dad when he was alive, and it was just fitting to keep doing it now. In all my sister's sincerity, she delivered the message, through tears, because Jeff couldn't be at the funeral.

When Mom chose individuals to participate in Dad's celebration, she selected people who truly knew Dad's heart, not his profession. Leonard Wheeler, retired NFL player and close friend, gave the greeting. Miki Kornegay had been a friend since 1987, and she sang an original song. Qadry Ismail, retired player and friend, read scripture. Roderick Barnes, close family friend, gave the acknowledgments. Vaso Bjegovic, close friend since 1994; Phil Pulido, close friend since 1998; Bill Horn, close friend; Todd Scott, retired NFL player; and Keith Jackson, one of Dad's best friends and retired Eagles and Packers player, all gave remarks. Bebe Winans, nationally known gospel singer and friend since 1986, sang "Stand," which moved Mom to tears. Keith Johnson, friend and Hebrew partner, gave Dad's eulogy and blessing. Finally, Shelley Barrow, friend and wife of NFL player Michael Barrow, did a praise dance that made Mom cry.

During Miki's musical selection, I looked around the altar of this beautiful church. I reflected on how it had been a while since I really was in church for a service. Until around eighth grade, our family were "normal" Christians. I had been under a roof like this before, with the high ceilings, with people praising and worshiping God but still not having peace in their lives. As a kid, I only learned what I like to call "the basics" of living for God. Before Dad's deeper study of the Bible, church was more of a norm rather than a way of life. I went to church when I was younger, either because it was Sunday or because my dad was preaching in some city every week during the off-season.

My eyes shifted, and I saw the Torah scroll laying on my father's casket. I saw the prayer shawl on his shoulders. I saw the shofar leaning against an enormous casket, and I thought, "That is my church, that is my fellowship, that is my belief." I realized then that what my dad had taught me in the last four years was more important than how many times I went to church. It was more important than being able to win Bible awards at school. It was more important in my dad's eyes to obey the commandments and live for God than going to a building where I'm not growing in God. Sure, a building could have been the haven for my learning, but it was not. When I looked at the shofar, the prayer shawl, and the 400-year-old Torah scroll, I knew that my dad had implanted the belief in my heart. It wasn't a place to go as I had gone for 12 years; it was a way of life that I had learned since then. It was God's commandments, and obeying those commandments that make people who they are in God, not the building or the church or even the people. My dad helped me to realize that even though he faithfully went to church all of his life until I was 13, and even though we were actively involved with God, that wasn't enough. We had to obey him and make obedience a way of life, not a building you go to on Sunday or a preacher you hear on Wednesday nights.

And as I looked at the man lying in the casket, I had only one regret. We had not always been as close as we had been in the last seven months. He was a father and he was a great one; but he wasn't always around because of his obligations to the world. Preaching and football. And after he retired, it was too late for him to easily build a relationship with me. It took him time and a lot of practice to really connect. Our relationship had just started to grow.

After the funeral, I had been very excited to see Brett Favre, Leroy Butler, Michael Strahan, James Brown, Bruce Smith, Eugene Robinson, and every other football player who had come to the funeral, but I didn't get to see them. My mom had arranged after the funeral for a separate room for them to eat and socialize with one another, along with close family and friends while everyone else was waiting to go over to the gravesite. Instead of sealing myself off, I went to see all of my friends I hadn't seen in years. Once again, I didn't want to be separated from the regular crowd.

In talking to my old friends, I realized that something strange was going on. Many of the people I was talking to, friends from Tennessee, friends from New Jersey, and friends from Green Bay, were all telling me that my dad had been in contact with them within the past month to just say hello. If everything else wasn't baffling enough that week with the dream and the tsunami, this was one of the strangest. My dad had contacted 80 percent of the families that had come to the funeral all within the month before he died. That was testament to my mom and me, especially after she checked the phone bill for verification, that we reasoned he knew he was going to die. He didn't know exactly when, but he knew it was coming.

Sitting around the kitchen table, I learned that Dad had called Mr. Garcia that month. He hadn't wanted anything in particular, just to say hello because it had been awhile. Art Moore called him, saying, "I love you, that's all I wanted to say, but I got to run." Then Robert Brooks said Dad had called him, too. Then I started asking around, and sure enough, him too, and her too.

We were always close to John and Kelly Caras and their son and daughter, Kasey and Katie. My cousin, Morgan, always loves a photo opportunity.

Dad had said, "Bonita, you know what I've realized? People don't have to know Hebrew to be in right standing with God. All they have to do is keep the Commandments." Knowing Dad came to that conclusion after years of eight-hour days studying Hebrew helped put my heart at peace. He had figured it out. I, on the other hand, had heard this repeated, but every Bible study he just found a different way to say it. When he wasn't saying it, he was just talking about the "did you know" factors of the Bible. For a long time Dad was lonely in his walk, and for him to come steadily to that simple, yet direct conclusion before he died made all of his studying that much more rewarding, for us all.

I would go on to get hundreds of sympathy letters from people extending their condolences and offering comfort. People I barely knew at school contacted me. The RA who flipped out when he first saw my dad moving me into my dorm even gave his respects. I had so much love and support and that eased my father's death. At a time that I should have felt most alone, I wasn't. All those people coming in and out of my house that week helped me process. The shared experience helped us all.

I think about him every day, and the thing I miss the most is the "what could have beens" because we were getting so close. We had just started to bond. I was never mad at God, and I never verbally asked why. I trust God in all that he does, and I know my dad was ready. I know that one day I will see him again, and that is all that matters. Until then I want to be able to get married, have a job I enjoy, and have kids of my own to whom I can tell great stories about their Granddaddy. Stories like this one, about a son who is taking giant leaps to leave a similar impression in his father's footsteps. Who'd have thought?

3

Conceived in August 1985, at the annual Copeland family reunion and born on May 12, 1986, was a seven-pound, eight-ounce boy named Jeremy Reginald White.

When mom was pregnant with me, she was in the Army. I still tell people that I was in the Army. Technically, since I was inside my mom when she was a part of the Army, then I was in the Army. Too bad I can't say I served already. When Mom had to serve her two summer weeks in the Army, Dad was on his own with me. Mom was an Officer in the Reserves until 1988. But he had a little help; Uncle Mark and my cousin Chris were there.

Mom loved everything about the Army. If she hadn't met Dad, she probably would have gone active duty out of college. She loved her peers, the Sergeant Major, the athletic training. She became a Second Lieutenant in May 1985. In January 1985, three days before she married my dad, her Colonel cleared her to go into the Reserves. She retired in 1988, just after Jecolia was born. She couldn't maintain her training and be an active mother/football wife simultaneously.

We never really believed that she could be recalled until she was 40; but we teased her about it all the time. The only time it was scary

I was always a happy baby.

was in 1991, when her unit, 677 Supply Company was activated for Operation Desert Storm. Mom sat in front of the television watching her friends, her brothers and sisters, preparing to go to war.

Before I was born, Dad wanted to name me Reggie. Now that would be cute and sweet if my dad never became the Reggie that everyone knows him for, preaching and sacking. If my dad would have played his "manly trump card" and insisted my name be Junior, my life would have been completely different. In the first place, there would be no room for trying to "cover it up." While there are many Reggies and innumerable Whites, it is difficult to go anywhere where no one knows who Reggie White is. When most of the places I lived were predominantly Caucasian and the teacher called on me, the only black kid in class, that's too much of a coincidence, even if my name was James or Robert. Think Green Bay, Wisconsin.

Uncle Mark, my grandparents, and my dad place second-lieutenant bars
on my mother's shoulder.

I love my dad, but I am glad that my mom changed his mind
on that matter. I am honored to be his son and to have his gifts as
a father; but his name might have changed who I became. I would
never have been able to escape the criticism of not playing football, and I would have been labeled stuck up and whatever else
people might speculate about me, because I am a famous person's
son.

Ultimately, Dad understood, and he settled for using "Reginald"
as my middle name. I like it. It is unique, yet not embarrassing to
tell to my friends.

When I was born there were complications: one that would not
hinder my living, and one that by the world's standards would hinder my living greatly. I tried to come out feet first instead of head
first. That was not a big deal, the doctors did what they do, and they
got me out fine through a c-section. Mom says I caused her great
pain for one month, but never since. I think that's a good trade. The

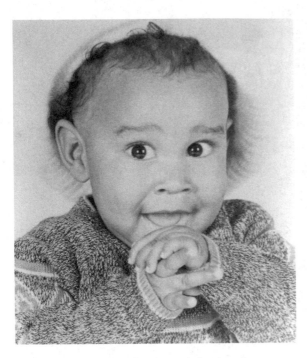

I was always posing for a photo. My mom loved to take pictures.
She probably has 500 of them in a box ready for scrapbooking.

second complication was that I was born completely deaf in my left ear (although they wouldn't find this out for a few months). Outside looking in, my parents and others probably cried and wondered how I would get through life with only one good ear. That will be answered throughout this entire story.

By the time I was born, the USFL had taken a downfall and was nearing its end. Many players from teams across the nation went to the NFL, my dad, of course was one of them. He had signed with the Philadelphia Eagles. Since he was a rookie, he was asked to sing a song in the locker room. Wearing a black and white sweatsuit with a microphone holder in front of him, he was trying to act like Elvis Presley with the pelvic thrusts and moves. Many of his teammates were laughing. To experience his singing (on tape, of course, I was too young to remember it first-hand) was funny; but his draft would change my life forever for the good and for the ugly, but not necessarily the bad.

When I arrived into the world, I was quite an adjustment on my parents. In the middle of the night when I was four months old, my mom was nursing me in their bed (OK, so I don't remember this—I'm taking my mom's word for it). They were exhausted, as all new parents are, and Mom and I fell asleep. Unbeknownst to me, the tide was shifting. Literally. In his sleep, Dad rolled over on top of me. Mom heard a breathless grunt and woke with a start. She shoved Dad off me, and I didn't sleep in the bed with them again.

When I was three months old, I seemed to want to wake up at 4 a.m. I didn't understand that was an unearthly time to awake, but Dad would remind me from their room. He hollered, "Jeremy, lie down. Go back to sleep." While I didn't have any control over whether or not I fell asleep, I would obey my father and lie back down, awake; but I didn't make a peep. About 7 a.m. Mom would come to start my day. From a very early age I had fear and respect for my father's words. However, sometimes the idea of lying back down stunk to me, literally. Once my dad told me to lie back down, and I did so in my own filth. But hey, when dad said something, I listened.

I do not remember this distinctly, but at 18 months, I had to go to the hospital and get tubes put in my ears. This surgery caused the doctors to discover the deafness in my left ear. My parents were devastated to learn I had no nerve endings in that ear. A hearing aid wouldn't help.

Mom and Dad did all they could to help me hear in my left ear. The only thing they could do now was pray. Nearly every time I went to church, the congregation prayed for my ear, and I remember my parents constantly praying for me at home. They knew God was going to perform a miracle and heal my ear so that I could hear out of it. When I was five years old, my mom and dad were very hopeful and faithful that my ear would be healed. At a healing service at a church in Tennessee, people were being slain in the spirit, or falling backward because they felt the presence of the Holy Spirit. As a five-year-old, I thought it was normal and told my mom I wanted to be healed. Little did my parents know I just wanted to "fall out" when the spirit moved me. She and my dad walked me up to the front of the church. All the while people were wailing and crying and saying they were feeling the presence of God. The preacher pulled me to him, and I looked behind me to make sure there was someone behind me to catch me. I felt ready, because this was the point where I was going to get to fall and someone was going to catch me. From my mom and dad's point of view, it was possible to have a miracle happen, and they hoped that the Holy Spirit would touch me. So, imagine my parents praying hard for their son's hearing to be healed, and their son waiting for the right time to take a dive. As the preacher put his hand on my forehead (and frankly, pushed me backward), I fell. When the usher caught me and lay me gently on the ground, I thought to myself, "Wow, this is cool, but it's kind of dark. I'll just open my eyes a little". I opened one eye to peek around to see what everyone else was doing. At that moment, my dad shot me a glance and saw my opened eye. He nudged my mom and whispered, "Look at Jeremy." They just stared at me. Then both of them burst into silent laughter. They realized that I was just doing it because everybody else was doing it, not because I was slain in the spirit. The praying helped, but not in a way that one would imagine.

I was a clumsy little guy. Often, I used to hurt myself falling. Whether it be falling down the stairs, on the ground, on the sidewalk, or off a bike. When I was four years old, I fell and hit my head on the stairs leading to our basement. My dad heard me cry, and he said, "Jeremy, what happened?!" Through tears I said, "I hit my head on the stairs!" He said, "Which stair did it?! Which stair hurt you?!" Blurry-eyed I said, "That one," and I pointed at the one I hit my head on. He said, "This one!?" And then he started to hit it. "Don't *hit* you *hit* my son! You hear me!" And I couldn't help laugh. My dad always had a way to get us to stop crying. As I got older, though, his creativity started to dwindle, and things that used to make me laugh didn't make me laugh so much anymore. But I always appreciated those moments when he tried.

I remember a school called Little Red School, although until yesterday while researching for this book, I thought it was named Little Big School. Little Red School was a Mothers' Morning Out. Mom didn't want me in day care much, but she did send me when I was three for some kiddie socialization and for her to have time to clean, shop, and go to her second home: the post office (My mom spent a lot of time at the post office throughout my life. She collected the fan mail, she kept up with Dad's preaching or appearance dates, and she accounted for all the money people would donate when Dad's hometown church was burned down. Mom even gathered all the hate mail we received after Dad spoke to the Wisconsin Legislature.).

She was often asked why she did not get a nanny for my sister and me. She always responded with authority. She did not want someone else raising her kids. My sister and I are fortunate that my mom was able to be a stay-at-home mom because she did exactly that: she raised us. Mom is very up front about her beliefs on parenting. She often says she knows billionaires who have several children, but they also have several nannies. She is adamant that they aren't raising their kids, the nannies are. Although Dad wasn't the one advocating mothers staying home, he did agree that parents should be the ones rearing their own children. Later, during the summer before college, I worked at Gateway Day Care with toddlers. I was one of only two guys who worked there, but I loved the kids. It was the best job I had to date. To play with the little kids all day and hear how funny they were was great. I loved them while I was there, but I was not sad to see them go home every day. I came home one day telling Dad about little kids being there all day. He just shook his head and said, "It's a shame people can't be home with their kids. Why would they want to leave their kids in day care from 7 a.m. until 6:30 at night?" We understood that some parents must have their children in day care full-time, but we were saddened by the families that used day care only to have "me time."

Little Red School was a fun place. We colored, we played, we did things little kids would do. I loved hanging out with my best buddy, Daniel Wehner. But my mom knew that this little boy was not a good influence and did not want me interacting with him when I was "impressionable," so she switched my day care days to Tuesdays and Thursdays, while Daniel was going on Mondays and Wednesdays. Slick, Mom, really slick. Daniel is not a bad guy now, he was just a mischievous little boy at the time. I was holding my

My mom took a photo every first day of school. Shari, Jecolia, and I were headed to our first day at Green Bay Christian in 1997.

own at two years old, but quickly came the news of a new chapter in my life. My baby sister.

A wonderful and memorable…well, I don't remember it, moment in my life is when my baby sister Jecolia (JAH-KOHL-EE-A) was born in New Jersey. Jecolia Regara (pronounced REGJARA for Reggie and Sara) White was born on May 24, 1988. Only two years and 12 days after my birth. From what I understand, I loved my sister immediately. I wasn't jealous of her at all. We used to play around when we were little. She was my baby sister and I was her big brother. And that is how it would be forever.

From what my mom tells me, the day my sister was born, I stayed at the house of our friends, John and Lisa Campiglia. People might have thought that I would have caused a lot of destruction because I was two and "I was away from my parents and could do whatever I wanted while at someone else's house." On the contrary, I have always listened to other people's parents as if they were my own, and even at two years old, it was no different. One morning John told me, "Now, Jeremy, it's not time for you to get up yet, you go back to bed, buddy." And sure enough, all I said was, "OK, John," and I went back to sleep. The next morning John entertained me with a bowl of cereal, some milk, a seat, and a television with those fabulous cartoons. I could watch cartoons for hours, and that still has not changed. In the midst of my sister's birth, my mom was away from mom duty for two whole days. This, however, did not stop my dad from being the responsible dad that he was called to be. The man did not change me into a new pair of clothes for two days straight. I guess I should be thankful that I later learned to dress myself.

When Jecolia was no more than six months old, I remember my dad trying hard to get my sister to smile at him. He would blow on her belly, try to tickle her nose with his face, and anything else he could think of to get an infant to laugh. My dad would keep telling me to "step aside" so that he could have Jecolia to himself for a moment. At only two years old, I did not understand this so I tried to get Jecolia to laugh myself. I thought I could help him out, but I didn't understand why he wouldn't let me try. I wiggled in and gave her a kiss on the cheek. Lo and behold, Jecolia cracked a smile. And not just any smile, I might add, this was an ear-to-ear smile.

My dad was not too happy about this, and it showed when I put my foot in his face. This could have meant a number of things. I either wanted him to smell my foot, take off my shoe, observe my shoe, tie my shoe, or maybe I was just doing it to be like "In yo' face, Daddy-o, I got my sister to smile." He did not realize what was happening because he was still trying to get my sister to laugh. And he said in his deep and commanding voice "Getcho foot outta my face!" The video my mom taped of this scene captured a very funny "Dad-losing-it moment," but watching in my teen years caused Dad to apologize.

I always knew that Jecolia was the baby so she was able to get away with things. When I was five and she was three, she used to do things to provoke me; and, of course, I would get in trouble for responding. This would mark the start of a new character trait that I would come to learn as "patience."

I'm proud to say that my sister did teach me a thing, actually two. My three-year-old sister taught me how to tie my shoes. And two years later she taught me how to snap my fingers. To this very day I tie my shoes the exact same way she taught me how to. Not with the criss-cross, no no no. I do the two bunny ears, which many consider the more difficult variation. But it gets me along just fine. It is just amusing that I have my sister to thank for this, and I will pass this method along to my own children one day.

On the subject of younger siblings, I have two other cousins who were coincidentally born in the same year as my sister. They were born to my mom's two older sisters. Shari (SHAH-REE) was born May 22, 1988. She is cool; she liked to play video games and we could battle together when I was younger. Wesley, who was born July 15, 1988, is the only boy who is younger than I. This was great because, at times, I got to be like a big brother to three baby siblings. But at times this was the worst thing in the world, because I got to be like a big brother to three baby siblings.

Growing up I was told to listen to my parents, because they'd know what is good for me. In case I needed a little coaxing, I was then introduced to what was called the belt whoopin'. For the politically correct and judgmental about this form of discipline and punishment, let me say right now that this was not abuse. My dad never punched me, slapped me, pushed me, kicked me, hit me across the face, in the stomach, under the chin, nothing. The only place he ever whooped me was on the behind. Frankly, I think God gave us cushion in our butts because when we need to be punished the whoopin' will not be so bad.

My sister and I were at Wesley's house visiting for a week in Ohio. My mom and Aunt Maria decided to leave us with the dads while they went to a spa. We got up and I was excited because I was visiting my cousin Wesley and I was in Ohio. We all woke up about the same time, I had some eggs, and I was ready to face the day. The first order of business: to go downstairs to Wesley's Sega Genesis and to play some Sonic the Hedgehog, gotta love it. But wait, what's this? The dads had something to say to the kids. We padded over dutifully. "OK, you all are done with breakfast, now go take a nap," Dad commanded. A nap!? It's 9:30 in the morning, and we just got up 30 minutes ago! I wiped my eyes and stared at him. There was no arguing with him, and my uncle has a stare that could kill a yak, so the three of us decided that it was in our best interest to go back to bed. We went upstairs and fell asleep, score one for the dads.

Actually, sending us to bed wasn't so different for Jecolia and me. When Mom left Dad in charge, he was not really active. We didn't go hiking or biking, because Dad was always saving his strength for Sunday's game. Instead, we might go to the mall or the movies, or he would come to one of our sport events.

Growing up in New Jersey was a new experience for me. I was young and beginning to make my first group of friends. When I was younger I loved to just sit in my mom's lap and lie on her chest and listen to her talk. It would calm me, and I used to be so intrigued by the sound. I was an amazed three-year-old.

Dad was asked a lot how he could play football on Sundays. Instead of the guilty reply they were often expecting, the answer was quite the opposite. Dad was always defending his playing on Sundays. Football was his job. Sunday or not, God knew his heart; and Dad wanted to perform the gift God gave him. The irony was some of those people asking were going to work on Sundays after church as well. Playing football on Sundays was no different then.

From that time on I started going to all Dad's home games. Sometimes my sister went when she got older, but there was a time in Green Bay that she'd rather play with her dolls at the neighbor's house than watch football, so she missed a few. We missed a lot of kickoffs, but Mom and I were always, always at the games.

One game in particular that I was amazed by as I got older was an Eagle divisional game against the Redskins. My dad scored a touchdown. He said, "Against Washington. I went for the sack, and all of a sudden the ball ended up in my hands, and I just ran for a touchdown." After seeing the video clip when I was older, I couldn't believe my eyes. Here was a 295-pound man running like he was being chased by alligators. He would eventually tell me also that he was sucking on an oxygen mask after that play. I just wish I was old enough to have seen it in person.

Another Eagles game I wish I had been older to appreciate was when Mom was enraged at another fan. The team wives sat together; and simply put, the wives on the Philadelphia Eagles team were united. If something bad happened to one of them because of someone else, the rest of the wives would have her back. One time an inebriated fan was smoking a cigarette and the smoke was bothering a pregnant Melanie Carter, Cris Carter's wife. Several of the wives asked her nicely to put out the cigarette. The fan didn't respond so nicely and a fight ensued. One of the Eagles wives punched the lady. As she rolled down the stands, the wives took turns hitting her. My mom was no different. During the fight, Mom had secured my three-year-old head in a football hold; my legs were swinging behind me. My mom was suffering from what we affectionately call the "Cleveland Reaction"; she sucker punched the woman as she fell across Mom's lap. Later, when my dad heard the story he could only laugh. It is often said you can take the woman out of the "hood" but you can't take the "hood" out of the woman.

As a youngster I was extremely interested in learning the "whys" to many of life's questions. Why is the sky blue? Why do we call a bed a bed? Why does a bike have two wheels? I used to ask my mom why a lot. Finally, one day, and I do not know whether she was fed up with it or she really was serious, I asked her why a television is what it is. She told me that it just is. From that point, I realized that my mom would not be able to answer all of life's tough questions, so I decided to back off for a while, just look at things, observe them, and learn. I learned early not to go against my parents and always tell the truth. There were also many times I would ask my dad questions and he couldn't answer. I used to ask him how he thought Moses might have reacted to seeing television today, or what Jesus' favorite food might have been. Because he couldn't answer, I told him, "When I get to heaven, I'm going to ask God all the questions you can't answer." He immediately replied, "God doesn't have time for all your questions, Jeremy." He didn't mean that God couldn't do anything, but, good grief, I had a lot of questions. He would definitely recant on that statement were he here today; but to be in his shoes with an overeager six-year-old wanting to know the mysteries of the world, I'm sure he felt that even God Himself didn't have enough time for my many questions.

Bedtime Bible stories told by a bear singing, "It's Beary Bear's, very best, bedtime Bible stories for you!" My mom used to pop it in the cassette player so that my sister and I could listen to them so many times. But it never ceased to entertain us before we went to sleep. There was also a Bible story book that looked like a regular Bible but with illustrations. When we heard the story about Noah's Ark, I looked at the illustration with pigs and other animals drowning. This blew my mind because I thought only people died, and that all the animals were saved. I couldn't grasp that "two by two" meant "only two lucky animals were awarded the honor of being the sole survivors of the species to repopulate the earth." At four, I felt

My dad always used to love taking my sister out on dates.
This was one of the 'casual' nights.

like the illustrator had made a mistake. I learned the shocking truth, and it was tough at first, that God let all those innocent animals die. Soon, I understood that when God does things He knows what He's doing.

4

I went to Lambs Road School in kindergarten, a rather small, mostly elementary school. If I spoke out of turn or jumped out of my seat or disregarded the teacher's direction, I would get my name written on the board. Two checks by my name would mean something bad, but it would never go that far. If my name was written on the board once, when I got home I would be whooped or get a talk, depending on what misdeed I committed. Only one time I got a stiff talking-to. Remember how when you raise your hand to a teacher and she clearly sees it but doesn't call on you? I hated that even as a five-year-old. I kept holding up my hand; but my teacher wouldn't call on me, so I put my hand in her face. Yeah, yeah well you're not supposed to do that, apparently.

Once in first grade I didn't get my name written on the board; however, my sister, who was in Pre-K, did. Getting into the car, I was so happy to tell my dad that I hadn't had my name written on the board. He said, "Good, Jeremy." Still, I felt bad because I knew my sister had her name written on the board and she was probably going to get in trouble. When my dad asked her, she said, "No." And he said, "Good, Jecolia." I looked at my sister and was shocked that she had lied. I had never lied to my parents, and I waited for a

Emmitt loves Dad so much that he actually put on the big 92. I had his jersey since I was in junior high school. I wore my jersey even on Packer Day at school.

voice from above to call her on it. We weren't supposed to lie to Mom or Dad for any reason. For a six-year-old kid to have this mind set is pretty good, if you ask me.

The uneasiness on my face told Dad to ask her if she was certain she didn't have her name written on the board. She gave in, and then the worst came. At this point, I was happy to be on the other side of the fence. The good side of the fence. The not-lying-to-my-

Kristen Singletary (Mike and Kim Singletary's oldest) and
I take a break after a long swim at our Pro Bowl hotel.

daddy side of the fence. Dad said she was getting a whooping. And
not just any old whooping. She was getting whooped with a switch
three whole times. I wasn't allowed to watch, but I was glad not to
be in her shoes. My sister only got whooped with the switch twice
in her life. Once was for the situation just described, and the other
was for cutting off a piece of her ponytail. My mom would tell us
not to do something, and my dad was the disciplinarian. Was I
going to question him? I think not.

But my mom was just as tough when she needed to be. At a
game against a divisional rival, an overeager fan asked Dad to
sign her butt with my mom and me standing right there.
Because Dad was speechless for a moment, Mom found his
words for him. She looked at that young woman and said, "No,
he's not going to sign your butt. His family is standing right here
with him. That is not OK." The first time I ever saw my mother
get mad in public or at home taught me not to mess with her
either.

That year we went to the Pro Bowl, and a couple of Hawaiian teens asked me if I was Reggie White's son. When I said yes, they asked me for my autograph. I didn't want to disappoint "the fans," so I took the slip of paper and commenced to drawing scribbles on it. I thought it looked pretty good. Authentic. They looked at the paper, then back at me like I had lost my mind.

From very early on, I had a favorite football player and a favorite football team. My favorite team was, and still is, the Dallas Cowboys, and that player was, and still is, Emmitt Smith. Surprising, I know. When I was about six years old, we went to the Pro Bowl and I had met Emmitt the year before. When I passed by him again that year he said, "Hey, Jeremy." I immediately skipped to my mom, yelling, "Mr. Emmitt remembered my name!" My mom says that's when she realized why people reacted the way they did when they met her husband.

While I was elated to meet Emmitt Smith at the Pro Bowl when I was six, I got my first inkling at ten of what other people must have

I am with my first girlfriend, Gina Campiglia. Our families vacationed together even after we left the Eagles.

I am always in the pool. Because we traveled so much with
ministry and football, my sister and I became fish.

felt like when they saw my dad. Again at the Pro Bowl, I was swimming in the pool at the hotel where all of the NFL players and families stayed. As I came up, I saw Deion Sanders walk by, and I was star
struck. Although I didn't chase him down, I wanted to. I remember
thinking, "Oh, this is what it's like for fans when they see Dad." I said
to one of my friends, "Hey, that's Deion Sanders!" My friend said to
me, "What are you talking about, man? Your dad is Reggie White!" I
was thinking to myself, Who cares? That's Deion Sanders!

My first grade teacher, Ms. Topi told us that we could not use our
fingers to add or subtract. We were supposed to use crayons or pen-
cils or pens. I tried to do this, but it took too long. When Ms. Topi
came by, I would count with my crayons, but the moment she left, I
would pull up my fingers and count away. To this day, when I count
for simple things, I use my fingers. Maybe if I had listened to Ms.
Topi, I would be a math whiz today. I hate math.

I was good, however, at something else in elementary school. I
was a Bible-verse memorizing machine. The first scripture I memo-

rized was Philippians 4:13, which states, and I proudly quote, "I can do all things through Christ who strengthens me." I would always win awards for memorizing the most Bible verses throughout the first half of the year. And yes, I still have the two trophies I won in kindergarten and first grade. Superheroes' kids often have their parents' powers, and I was no different. I got my Bible verse-memorization skills from my dad. When I got older, I could always ask him, "Where does it talk about Jesus' second coming?" And he could rattle off a few specific verses. Presently, I'm not as good as he was, but he studied the Bible a lot longer than I have, but I still have his genes.

A girl in my first grade class, named Holly Ryan, was supposed to be my girl. Another girl in the class, Bethany, would ask, "Jeremy, who are you going to marry, Holly or me?" And, being the truthful playa that I have always been, I said, "Holly." But I liked the girls. When I was younger I had several girlfriends. There was Holly, a girl named Gina Campiglia (John and Lisa's daughter), and Raven Simone from *The Cosby Show* (although Raven didn't know she was my girlfriend). Two of my father's teammates' wives were also my girlfriends. I wasn't partial to any one race or age; they were all great. One day while we were watching *The Cosby Show*, I told my dad, "That's my girlfriend," (I was six at the time). He said, "Jeremy, how many girlfriends do you have?" I told him I had five. He said, "Five? You can't have five girlfriends. You have to pick one." I thought about it and said, "OK, I want Gina to be my girlfriend." I had chosen the most beautiful girl who walked the face of my first-grade planet. I thought I would actually have a chance with Gina when I got older.

Gina Campiglia is a beautiful Italian girl who still lives in New Jersey. Our families have been good friends since we lived there. Although I had chosen Gina, who is four years older, as my girlfriend, I don't think she knew, but she did find out. Maybe it was my mom and dad telling her parents that we were betrothed, or maybe it was all those times when I was five or six giving her random kisses on the cheek and watching her giggle and smile. It was easy to sweep in because when I was six and she was ten, we were the same height. She is now 4-foot-10 and more beautiful than ever. I have such a weakness for older and shorter women. Oh yes, the older women are all right with me.

In my early childhood I loved to go over to Gina's house or for her to come over mine. She, my sister, and I played house. It was simple: Jecolia as the daughter, me as the father, and Gina as my lovely wife. We probably did things like going to work, cooking, cleaning, and disciplining our daughter, although not for real. One day at Gina's house, I wanted to tie up their cat with a jump rope. I wasn't trying to abuse it, I just wanted to tie its feet together. I realize that may sound like abuse, but I had it in mind to "rope" it like cattle.

Needless to say, the jump rope got wrapped around its neck and it started getting short on air. My six-year-old brain believed a normal mammal would stop and try to get it off. But not this crazy cat, it ran all over the house hissing and making cat noises, definitely not meows. Gina's parents got involved and held down the cat. Gina's mom, Lisa calmed the cat down and took off the rope. I felt bad, but I was more embarrassed because Gina was my future wife. I hoped she did not think that I would treat our pets, or possibly kids, like that. OK, so I didn't think that way when I was six, but I still felt bad. After all the madness, I still had my girl and she still loved me (I did see the cat a month ago and we are cool...and yes, it is still alive...amazing).

When my parents had to attend speaking engagements, Jecolia and I had free range at home. Actually, we had a darn good babysitter who played Twister and watched cartoons with us. Heather, Daniel the bad toddler's older sister, babysat us in Jersey. She was 13, and she let us stay up later than our parents said (sorry, Mom). When Heather noticed Mom and Dad coming home, she would say, "Jeremy and Jecolia, it's time for bed, your parents are pulling up." Then my sister and I sprinted upstairs, hopped into bed, and let out a little giggle because we thought our parents never knew what Heather was letting us do. Thinking about it today, they probably did.

There was a time when Heather actually put her foot down. My mom had this unbelievable fetish with having my sister and me constantly wear lotion (this fetish has not gone away). After I got out of the bathtub one night, Heather told me to put on lotion, so I doused myself. She took that as a mocking slap in the face, and she told me, "Jeremy, I'm going to come back in here in two minutes, and if you do not have all that lotion rubbed into your skin by the time I get back, you are going to be in trouble, and you can't use a towel!" I was frantically rubbing my legs and arms to get my skin to drink the massive amounts of lotion that I had put on. I think I got it all in, without using a towel, because I did not get in trouble.

The most vivid memory I have of Heather babysitting us is when I almost died. Well, actually, I didn't almost die, but I was extremely embarrassed. Whether I was hurt is open to speculation, even for me. At six, I decided to look down from the top bunk to show my sister that I could. The only part of me on the bed was from my waist down; the rest of me was hanging over the edge like a crazed monkey. Daring. There was some giggling, and then, to me, the strangest, unpredictable thing happened. Or, to someone else, the inevitable happened. I flipped over the side of the bunk bed and landed on my back. I was not necessarily hurt, but because I was a strong six-year-old boy who messed up in front of his four-year-old sister, I was embarrassed. I did the first thing that came to mind: I cried hysterically. Heather ran up and gave me some comfort, probably thinking I just fell off the bed, certainly unaware it was an accident that I caused.

Another great pastime for me as a kid was swimming. I was never scared to swim, and for some reason, I was like a fish; I never thought that I couldn't swim. I was a natural. The first day, my mom dressed me in a full-body swimsuit with about eight of those cylinder white things inside of the swimsuit to keep me afloat. When Tammy, my swim instructor, told my mom, "He can't wear these floaties," I was sad because we had spent ten minutes getting those floaties all in; and I was ready to swim. I knew it from the start: all it takes to swim is putting your arms out in front of you and rotating them while kicking your legs. When my dad would take us swimming I always tried to impress him with how well I could swim. He would throw things into the deep end of the pool, and I would retrieve them and come back to the top with no problem. He constantly told us not to run around the pool or to jump in right next to another person. He didn't want me to slip while running around the pool, and he didn't want me to hit someone else if I jumped on top of him or her in the pool.

Tammy's mom loved for Jecolia and me to come to her house and hang out. I played video games with her younger brother (I was a partial competitor even at six years old). My mom informed me that one day when she came to pick me up Tammy's mom, Lynn said, "Sara, I don't know what you did to that boy, but he is such an obedient child."

"What do you mean? What did he do?" My mom asked.

"I let him watch TV," she said, "I stopped at *The Smurfs* and said, 'Here, Jeremy, you can watch The Smurfs."

I knew my dad did not want me to watch The *Smurfs* because it had witchcraft in it. Papa Smurf had a black cauldron and would practice alchemy. His nemesis, Gargamel, cast spells. Dad had some beliefs he could waver on, but witchcraft was not one of them. I had told Ms. Lynn, "No, Ms. Lynn, I can't watch *The Smurfs*." I proceeded to cover my eyes until she turned the channel.

Maybe she just wanted to test out this obedience "act" to see if it was legit. She said, "Jeremy, your mom is not here, it's OK."

I quickly responded in all my six-year-old honesty with, "No, no Ms. Lynn, I can't watch *The Smurfs*." And literally, I turned my head while closing my eyes. This scene planted the seed that grew into an enormous trust my parents have in me. Many of my friends didn't experience such a trust, and I know that's why it was special.

My mom incorporated sports into my daily regimen early. I played pee-wee football and was an All-American six-year-old, playing the most obvious position, defensive end. Pause, think about it. I didn't play football! When I was six I played soccer. Soccer was my sport. On a team with orange shirts. We wore our orange shirts, drank Hi-C and ate oranges during halftime. Quite a theme. I always wondered what the team that wore black shirts got for half-time, coal? In that moment, I was happy to be an Orange.

I was always the kid in sports who never scored a goal, never made a huge contribution to the team, but would play hard, that is until I was tired, and then I would just stop and say I was finished. People knew me because my mom was always cheering for me on the sidelines and making certain each kid had a snack and water at each game.

Once we faced the black-shirt team, and on that day they did not have enough players. They asked if some of us wanted to play on the black team. I was thinking, let's just beat them; they don't have a lot of people and we'll win. Somehow I got on the black team. I think it was my mom—dang it, Mom. When I went to the black team, Daniel (the bad toddler who was now six) was still on my orange team. He was a ball hog and wouldn't pass anyone the ball. I was glad not to be on his team for the day. The coach for the other team said I was "running like a deer," and vigorously playing the role of a teammate on my new team. The only difference here was that I actually got the ball. I had the ball at midfield, and before you know it, I was at the goal. I wound up to kick and scored! Even my coach from the orange team was happy. I ran over to her, she picked me up, and I pumped my hands in the air like I had just won the Super Bowl, the NBA Finals, the World Series, and the Stanley Cup all in that same two seconds. It was one of the greatest experiences of my life; but it did always amaze me that the first goal I ever scored in my entire life was against my own team.

One reason my dad didn't come to many of my events was his job. Normally, Dad got up in the morning at 7 a.m. and was off to practice. He would return at 5 p.m. This happened on Monday, Wednesday, Thursday, and Friday. He only had Tuesdays off. On Tuesdays, he would head to workouts about 11 a.m. for two or three hours. Because Dad was at work, Mom, Jecolia, and I would go to soccer games or practices during the week. Whether the week's game was at home or away determined our family's Saturday schedule. If he played away, Dad left at 10 a.m. If the game was at home, he left at 7 p.m. for the local hotel with the team. Unfortunately, he was at practice and was never able to come to any of my soccer games when I was younger.

When my sister got a little bit older, around four, my mom decided she needed to play a sport. Jecolia would learn to be a team player, to know the fundamentals of a sport, to be competitive yet sportsmanlike, the whole nine yards. I was all for her playing a sport, except she was playing soccer. And if she was playing soccer, that meant, Lord help us, she was going to be on my team! At six, I realized that I would always be part of a team of at least two. I wouldn't get to be an individual, an only child. Someone would always be attached to me in some way, and that person was my sister.

At a soccer game, with the ball going right to left, up and down the field, I ran fast trying to score one for my team, and all of a sudden something great happened. The ball rolled right in front of my sister. But wait. What's this? The fans were screaming, "Kick the ball, Jecolia!" Then the craziest thing I ever heard was yelled by my sister, "Where is it?!" The ball was right in front of her, no more than about eight inches in front of her big left toe, and she didn't see it. For some reason, though, the other team didn't know what was happening. And when I yelled to her, she finally kicked the ball like little children do, and the ball went a whopping 12 inches. Thirty whole centimeters; but oh boy, a lot of millimeters. But, I would later understand, it's not about whether you win or lose, or if you even kick the ball, although she finally did. Later, she would grow up and play a little basketball. People were always scared of her because she clearly has my dad's genes to be tall and strong. Instead of the infamous words, "gettin' it from her mama," she got her athleticism from her daddy. Bless her heart, she looks like him too, she even got his nose.

Childhood memories would not be complete without two things: an extremely old stuffed animal that I've had my whole life and and remembering my first pet. My stuffed animal I received when I was just three years old was a Chow-Chow dog. I remember trying to think of a name, and looking around the room, I didn't want to name it dresser, carpet, wall, bed, sheets, light, counter, bulb, or anything like that. Then I saw it, a picture of my dad, mom, and myself at Sea World. I decided to name my stuffed animal "Picture." I still have that stuffed animal today. My dad always made fun of me as I got older and still took it with me places. He used to say, "I have a 13-year-old son who takes this daggone dog everywhere with him." I must say Picture made for a comfortable pillow on some long plane rides.

My sister and I were blessed to be able to have pets at a young age. When I was about six in New Jersey, Mom, Jecolia, and I went to the pet store to see all the puppies and dogs. They had a room in the pet store to take a dog and play around with him, kind of a test-me-to-see-if-you-want-me room. We went in and grabbed this puppy and that puppy. My sister and I had the time of our lives. My mom, whom I felt bad for, had to hold all the dogs herself and bring them into the test room. One dog she grabbed was a full-grown Dalmatian. This would have been all right if my mom had not had trouble with her back; and it also would have been OK if the Dalmatian had not been as excited as a life-serving convict who gets freed for a few days, no questions asked. The Dalmatian kicked and panted, and when we put it down, it was almost as long as the room. He was playing with the little ball we had for him, but I leaned over to my mom and said, "He's a nice dog, but he's too big." And inside I felt bad because I felt like we were leading on the dog. This dog was thinking it had a home, although we wanted nothing to do with it. After a bit more looking, we found two puppies: one Pomeranian and one Bichon Frise. Those were the two puppies we wanted. I wanted the Pom, and my sister wanted the Frise. We were asking for two puppies, but neither of us thought we would get those puppies because we had to run it by Dad first. And in cases like these the answer was always no. My mom's answer was a lousy, "We'll see." She was probably counting on him saying no. We went home, saying goodbye to the puppies.

We got home, and honestly, I don't remember if we asked Dad or not, but within the next week my sister and I came home from school to two lively puppies whining in a cage in my room. We let them out and started playing with them. My mom said, "What are you gonna name them?" I named the Pomeranian Sparkles. And since my sister was four, I took the liberty of naming the Frise Rainbow. From then on, Sparkles and Rainbow conquered the White world. I won't go into the details of us not walking them or potty training them for the longest time. Let's just say my sister and I were the designated "have fun with the dogs" crew, not the "take care of the dogs" crew. Give us a break, we were four and six.

When Jecolia and I played with our cousins, sometimes it got rough. Once, Wesley got mad at something and started crying. Jecolia and Shari weren't crying, but I was intrigued to see what it would be like for everyone to be crying. I was seven years old and they were five. I hit Jecolia and made her cry. And while Shari was looking at me strangely, I hit her and made her cry. With the resounding wails from the little kids, I stood back, observing. It wouldn't be long before the adults came in now. If they asked me about anything, I always told the truth. There was never a time they walked away from a situation not knowing what had happened. My mom, indeed, came in and asked us what happened so I told her that one of them was crying, and I decided to hit the rest of them to see what it was like to see them all cry. I think the reason I did not get punished was because it was just so strange. If my dad had known what I did specifically, I most definitely would have been punished.

While living outside of Philadelphia, my mom's brother, Uncle Mark, and my cousin Christopher lived with us. Every time I'd see my cousin Chris as I got older, he would always ask me if I wanted some juice and then laugh. Apparently when I was little I would always ask "iss" for some "uice." I was such a cute baby, but Chris at 15 didn't think so. It was nothing bad, Chris loves me and I love him, so it is all good.

Our grandparents, Uncle Mark, cousin Chris, Dad, Mom, Jecolia, and I are on our way to Pastor Bruce Sofia's church. He gave me my first stuffed animal, the chow I named Picture.

Uncle Mark used to sing Praise hymns to me like, "Lord, oh Lord, how majestic is your name in all of the Earth." But his singing was not done in a worshiping manner, it was just funny, even though he could hold a note. I remember coming back home one night to see him playing Nintendo; the original, another thing that changed my life. He was playing it and I wanted to play. He must have known that it was almost time for me to go to bed so he let me play. Lo and behold, my Mom called me and told me that it was time for me to go to bed. I was mad. I knew that I was the only one in the house who could challenge him to a game because I had been beating my dad at video games since I was three years old. It wasn't fair that I had to go to bed. But I obeyed and went to bed anyway.

Also, when I was younger, my dad always used to imitate people and act like he was them to fool us. Often, he would call home pretending to be his own idol, saying, "Hey, ya' see, Jeremy, ya' see, this is Bill Cosby, ya' see. And I'm calling you....to ask...if you...want a booowwwll of Jeeellloo puuudding!" And I would tell him, "Dad, I know this is you! Stop playing." He would say, "I'm not playing, I really just want to know if you want a bowl of Jello pudding, ya' see." I would go along with it some days, and other days I wouldn't. As I got older I realized that I also had his talent. I can't imitate Bill Cosby as well as he could, but I've found out that I can imitate a lot of people. I got that ability from him. And I love being able to do that.

5

During the off-season, we moved back to Tennessee. Mom and Dad wanted to have a home base, a place to have roots. Football wasn't forever, family is.

We lived on 30 acres. Before the house was built, I remember the grass was extremely long; so long that my three-year-old self could-n't see over it. My dad picked me up and put me on his shoulders. That one moment was symbolic of my life now in that he was able to lift me up to see and understand all on my own. And ultimately, I would be able to see things he couldn't, because he helped me get to where I am today.

Home life in Tennessee was something different than it was in Jersey or Green Bay. Not only did we not have any real neighbors because we lived on 30 acres; we were farther away from the people I went to school with. First Apostolic Academy was 30 minutes away from our house, and my classmates lived at least 45 minutes away. We had a satellite, one of the old ancient, huge, bulky satel-lites from way back in the day, and I would always watch the Cartoon Network, my favorite channel in the whole world. I would watch it for hours (sometimes eight) on end. The really long hours of watching it were usually during the summer when I was "on

Dad and I are ministering in a public school together. I always looked
forward to him calling me up to help him with his imitations. Jecolia
was always too shy, and Mom always had a camera.

vacation." I remember the old *Plastic Man*, *Snorks*, *James Bond Jr.*, all
the *Looney Tunes*, *Wacky Racers*, *Tom and Jerry*, and the now-Cartoon
Cartoons, which way back in the day were called World Premier
Cartoons, and the first ones were the *Power Puff Girls*, *Johnny Bravo*,
and *Dexter's Laboratory*; classic. I even remember the buttons to
press on the remote to call up the channel, because it wasn't like
satellite today where one can just scan the channels. We had to type

in the galaxy and then the channel, and there were like 16 galaxies, I think. Cartoon Network was Galaxy 1, channel 8.

When I was younger I also liked to watch movies. Disney, action, adventure, suspense, and comedies were a regular part of my viewing pleasure. One movie in particular my dad decided I could watch on my ninth birthday (because until then he thought it might be too scary for me) was *The Mask*. I was so happy to get that movie that I watched it nine times in three days. My dad would always joke with friends and say, "I finally let my son watch this movie, and he's watched it nine times in three days! Who watches a movie nine times in three days!?" I told him, "But Dad, it's *The Mask*. It's really cool!" Today, my total count is up to 33 times with my sister in second place with 27 times. We should be in a record book or something.

In Tennessee, I went to a school called First Apostolic Christian Academy. I attended that school during second semester until I was in the third grade. It was challenging to start to get to know people and to start my work each midyear. When we were in Jersey, I would go to Lambs Road; and then when I would get to Tennessee, I would go to First Apostolic for the second semester. So each January, I had to readjust. Thankfully, my mom is a smart woman. She picked schools both in Jersey and in Tennessee with the same curriculum: A-Beka-Books. A-Beka includes the same spelling words in the corresponding chapter of history or science. It was all interrelated and very beneficial for the student. Especially one who moves every six months.

My kindergarten teacher was Sister Philipia. We had to call all the teachers Sister or Brother since it was an Apostolic school. One day I really just wanted to stay home for a day. Mom let us skip a day and go to Show Biz Pizza Place, which now is called Chuck E. Cheese. We played Skee Ball and video games and ate nearly an entire pizza, then we came back home and went to school the next day like normal. I needed help with an assignment that the class had started the day I skipped off to Show Biz; and I said, "Sister Philipia, I don't know how to do this because I wasn't here yesterday." She said, "You shouldn't have been gone, Jeremy! Where were you?" And this is one of those times being a truth-teller wasn't so great. I replied, "I went to Show Biz." In a distinctive, forthright tone, she said, "How can you go to Show Biz and learn? You need to be able to *learn*, and you can't *learn* at Show Biz." When I got older, I told my mom that story, and she said, "Why did you tell her we went to Show Biz!?" I asked her if she wanted me to lie. She laughed, "No, but dang, she said it like that?!" And we just started laughing.

In second grade, I went to school one morning and the teacher asked her usual, "How are you this morning?" I guess I didn't want to give the standard "fine" reply, besides, I had something to share. "Dad broke the bed last night." Having stumbled upon a great story to tell for the rest of time, Sister Clapton said, "What?" I beamed, "Mom and Dad broke the bed last night." Little did I know that for weeks to come Mom and Dad would be teased. And teased. And teased. What I didn't know was Dad would go on to break several beds in his life, five to be exact. But in his defense, a 295 lb. defensive end can't just cannonball even onto the sturdiest bed. Slats are only so resilient. Also, what I didn't know was why everyone thought this was such a hot story. It wasn't until I was 18 and recalled the event with my dad that I realized what ridicule I had subjected Mom and Dad to.

Depending on the year and how much my dad had to preach, my mom would home school us the second semester of the school year. The half of the year he was not playing football, he was doing what he felt was more important, preaching. Our family traveled all over the country with him, either hitting or landing in nearly 40 of the 50 states for football and preaching. To really put into perspective how much we traveled: if we were home for ten or 12 days in a row during second semester when I was in grade school, then that was a good month. We were constantly living out of suitcases, flying practically everywhere. Another reason my sister and I had to grow up a bit quicker was there was no going to the kids' section of the church when my dad spoke. I probably heard him preach over 70 times. At seven years old, I could be caught mouthing the words my dad was preaching. Obey the commandments. People had to suffer to obey. People perished for lack of knowledge. Endurers of the word, if you love me, you'll obey my commandments. The list goes on.

Throughout the years I had come to memorize his sermons and his key points so well that every time he said, "And I'll end with this," I would lean to the person next to me and say, "Set your watch, we got another ten minutes," and it never failed. Every time he spoke, he always had a passion for preaching, and I enjoyed hearing him talk. There were many times he was concerned on what to speak about; but he said that God spoke through him, and I have no doubt about that. Whatever his message, Dad had such a vigor and such a passion for it that he would not just do the traditional topic, he had to go deeper than any preacher had ever spoken. When he spoke on faith, he enjoyed being able to delve deeper than a level of understanding. Most people would say that faith is the belief in things not seen. But Dad reveled in showing others the truth in the entire chapter of Hebrew 11 that clearly shows faith is obedience. It reads of Moses and Noah having faith because they obeyed God. While it is believing in something one doesn't see, it is much, much deeper. Actually obeying the commandments of the being that you cannot see fleshes out the definition of faith. And that kind of lesson would continue into his defining years as a man of God.

When I was younger, my dad always used to insert into his sermons why he was going to go to Heaven. He would become ardent, saying, "You know, I'm not going to be let into Heaven because I'm Reggie White. It's not like I'm going to get to the gates and see Jesus, and Jesus is going to say, 'Oh, my God! Hey! It's Reggie White. Reggie, you were the best defensive player of all time. You've been to so many Pro Bowls, and you've sacked so many quarterbacks. Man, you can go ahead and come on in! Hey! God! Yo, Dad! Get me a pen; Reggie White is here, and I want to get his autograph! Come on in, Reggie!" He said when he stands before God he knows it's not going to be for what he did, but for who he was as a person. Who was Reggie White? Was he a caring person, a mean person, a giving

We are celebrating because Dad finally decided for which team he'd be playing.

person, a selfish person? Depending on his relationship with God and who he was on this earth would decide whether he went to Heaven or not. He always wanted to be remembered for what he did off the field more than on the field.

During football season, Uncle Steve would take care of the Tennessee house. When we were there, he would take my sister and me to the mall or out to eat. Basically he would hang out with us when my mom had errands and my dad was working out. Uncle Steve was a main source of entertainment for my sister and me. He was always willing to lend a hand. My family paid him to do miscellaneous things around the house, and he was part of our family. Every time he and I walked outside to his car, he would say, "Jeremy, whose Cougar is that?" And I would say, "Uncle Steve, that's your Cougar." He would say, "That is my Cougar." He was proud of his car. One year, my parents bought him a white Explorer. He walked out back to where his Cougar was always parked and saw the new car. My parents had given me the keys to give him. And I said, "Hey, that's a nice car, huh?" And he said, "Yeah." I asked him whose it was, and he shook his head. I flashed the keys as cool as an eight-year-old could and said, "You want it, it's yours." Stunned, he thought I was kidding. I said, "No, it's yours." And from then on he would say, "Jeremy, whose Explorer is that?" And I would say, "That's your Explorer, Uncle Steve." I loved that my dad was always willing to help people who treated him like a human being and weren't trying take advantage of him. Because Steve was one of those people, my dad had no problem buying him a new Explorer.

One thing I never understood about Uncle Steve until I got older was his constant questions about what I learned in school. Instead of giving him specifics I would just name off my subjects. It used to get on my nerves, but I still told him most of the time. Now I realize he was trying to get me to bring my knowledge home, not leave it all at school. He was trying to teach me a great principle, lost on my young age.

My sister and I were home schooled during the second semester we'd come back from Green Bay. I was always a fast worker, and my mom would sometimes give us oral tests, which I feel were better than written tests sometimes. Not everyone tests the same way. It seems like more school systems would realize that; but at least for me, my mom did.

When I was seven or eight, a common question at school was "Do you get everything you want?" Dad's status in the community was already causing enough stress to me, that I didn't want to flaunt it further with mad possessions. I know it sounds impossible for a seven-year-old to think this way; but it's true. I used to stretch out

my tennis shoes instead of asking for a new pair. Just before I went
to public high school, I found that I needed some new clothes
because I was used to wearing uniforms for years. I asked for some
money to go shopping, and Dad said, "You gotta job?" Even then I
could wear a pair of jeans I had from the sixth grade. A little less
baggy and a little shorter, but they fit. I didn't care; I wore them. In
a high school with 2,000 other teenagers, no one would suspect the
highwater-jeans kid was Reggie White's son.

I was the King of Waiting; since my birthday was in May, I could
make it to Christmas (until we didn't have Christmas anymore). I
would get everything I needed or wanted then. And most of the
time because I wouldn't ask for things like clothes and some toys
and such, my mom would get me certain things she thought I needed (like new shoes for the ones I was stretching out). Also there was
something in our household called "Straight A coupons." Every time
we had straight A's on our report card, we got to spend them on
anything we wanted. Usually I would spend them on video games.
This is the reason my video game collection was so vast when I was
younger, because I made a lot of straight A's in elementary school.

With those A's came a lot of learning, and not necessarily the
school kind. When I was eight years old and my parents were
asleep, my sister, friend Erica Garcia, and I were playing at my
house. It was March, and we wanted to go swimming. Because we
had an indoor pool we didn't see the problem. I came to find out
there were two problems: the pool was not heated yet, and our parents did not give us permission. Uncle Steve was not about to defy
my parents and say what we could, especially with something like a
swimming pool.

My sister went upstairs and came back down, saying that my
mom said we could go swimming. I didn't know that she didn't really ask, because my mom was asleep. I only put my feet in because
the water was so cold; but my sister and Erica waded all over the
shallow end. I don't know how they just endured the cold water like
that. About 20 minutes later, Uncle Steve said, "Jeremy, Jecolia, your
mom and dad want to see you." I didn't know what we did, but I

knew that tone. In their room, all I saw was a woman lying in bed exhausted, and a man who wished he were lying in bed, red-eyed from lack of sleep. My dad said in a low, but understandable, voice, "Why were you guys in the pool?" And I said, "Jecolia told me Mom said it was OK." And he said, "Well, Jecolia, for lying you are getting a whooping."

She got four licks of the belt on her bathing-suit bottom. And I knew I was getting a whooping even though I didn't think I had done anything wrong. But my dad told me instead, "You didn't do anything wrong, but you are getting a whooping for believing a six-year-old." I did not understand it when I was younger, but my dad was teaching me that you cannot trust everyone even if he or she is close to you. One thing my dad always did after he whooped us was to ask us to tell him why we were whooped, then he would make sure he told us that he loved us and that he didn't like doing it, but he had to. I feel like I turned out fine, so it worked and I have an appreciation for it.

There was a swimming pool incident where I did do something wrong. I didn't get a whooping, but I should have. My cousin, Kiera did not like to swim unless she had a floatie. Since I knew every-thing, I said, "She's never gonna learn how to swim if she always has those on. I had to take off my floaties before I learned how to swim. If I learned how to swim by that time, she should too."

I was so stupid! But I decided to bring her over into the five-foot end of the pool and turn her loose. She straight sunk. I tried to pull her back up, and I couldn't. Thank God that Uncle Steve was there. He reached down there just as Kiera's face was starting to get red (because no doubt she was panicking), and he snatched her up. He yelled at me for it. And I was in a huffy-puffy mood because I didn't want to admit what I did was horribly wrong. But I had done it, and looking back, it could have ended a whole lot worse. Thank God for forgiveness and learning.

Our family also celebrated together. Birthdays were fun around my house, because my sister and I celebrated ours together since they are 12 days apart. One year my dad got us little tiny dirt bikes.

We always had to ride with our helmets on, but sometimes I got so excited that I just darted off without mine. When I would realize it, I would cut back to the garage so I wouldn't get in trouble. One day, when I did have my helmet on, I was driving around on our property in the grass. But I didn't see the hole in the ground. I was going about a good 15 miles per hour when I speared into the hole, went head first over the handlebars, bike following and flipping past me. All I could think about was how much trouble I was going to be in. I jumped up like nothing had happened when I saw my dad running toward me. All I could say was, "I didn't mean to, I didn't mean to." I was surprised to see all he was worried about was if I was ok. I said, "Yeah, I'm fine," and then, "I'm sorry." He hugged me and said, "Don't be sorry, I was just making sure you were OK." I'll never forget him running to me like that. He was so worried. That's one of the first times I saw Dad as someone other than a disciplinarian, someone in the pulpit, or a player on the football field. He genuinely cared for my well being. He was my daddy. He wasn't there just for scolding; he was there to protect and raise us to think for ourselves and to know right and wrong. He was my father.

6

While I did live in Tennessee until I was about ten years old, make no mistake about it, that is not what I consider my childhood. My childhood experiences are all attributed to the greatest small town on earth: Green Bay, Wisconsin. While I'm always asked, "So what's home to you?" every single time I give the same answer, "Green Bay." The next question is always how did I survive the cold weather. Heck, I was a kid, and I had cold weather in New Jersey, and I was just happy to be in Green Bay getting to know my friends, so I didn't care about the cold. I was forever in high gear, out the back door to the best sledding hill or to Adam's awaiting video game competition, with my mom constantly hollering behind me to put on a jacket.

All my childhood memories happened at 2910 Painted Trail Court. From Dad coming home after a long day at practice, to people driving around our neighborhood just to get a glimpse of where the great Reggie White lived. From kick ball to freeze tag, to endless hours of video games, Green Bay is forever my home. Everyone in the cul-de-sac knew each other, and for the most part, liked each other. The first day we moved in, I looked out of my mom and dad's bedroom window and saw three kids playing in their driveway. A

12-year-old, an eight-year-old, and the shortest and youngest was three years old. I said, "Mom, I wanna go meet them! I wanna play outside!" She told me there would be plenty of time to play outside but we needed to unpack.

Waiting is so hard for a seven-year-old. The first night we did not have beds and barely had covers, sheets, and pillows. The driveway kids' father gave us some pillows and extra covers, our first neighborly kindness. I had to sleep in the same room as my dad, and we slept on the floor that night. I knew Green Bay, Wisconsin, would be my home for a while. I could feel it.

The neighbors' oldest child, Adam, and I shared, and still do share, a common love for video games. Also he introduced me to Jackie Chan, Bruce Lee, Dragon Ball, Anime, and movies. Although there was a five-year age difference between us, we played video games together. Often it would only take one phone call. Within 15 seconds, we said all that needed to be said. To play or not to play.

And if he couldn't come over, usually he was about to have supper. He always said "supper", I said "dinner". We would play *Mario Kart*, *Street Fighter 2 Turbo*, *Skitchen*, *Earth Worm Jim*, *Sonic*, *X-men*, *NBA Jam T.E.*, the classic *Toejam and Eearl*, *Hockey*, *Madden*, *Tekken*, and *Golden Eye 007*. If it was popular, we were playing it. Even at 12 and seven, we were good competitors for each other. That's why video games are good for you, bringing friends together every day. And I can honestly say, this boy was my best friend growing up. He accepted me as younger, but still a fun guy. Later, he would be the first friend with whom I rode in a car without my parents. Adam is a great guy; and I didn't go on to make a lot of close male friends; they wer mostly female friends.

Another thing that Adam interested me in was reading. Not that I did not like to read before, but I was actually interested in reading about the video games I was playing. I had an opinion when I was younger that Playstation was the best system out there; now it was time to be able to back up my opinion by being able to subscribe to a magazine that provided information about video games. My mom had once made a deal with me that if it was reading material she would buy it for me. My dad didn't even know they made magazines devoted to video games. I couldn't wait for *Electronic Gaming Monthly* to come every month. I would read it from front to back and back to front again. I knew all there was to know about video games. I knew what was coming out a year and a half from the present date, and I was excited to prepare for its arrival. Later, inspired from this magazine, I decided for certain what I want to do with my life. Magazine writing and video games.

His parents, Todd and Beth Klarner, are people to emulate. Next to my own mom and dad, I want my future marriage to be similar to theirs. Never once have I seen them argue or seem angry with each other. If they do get mad, they have a good way of keeping it to themselves. My mother and father quickly trusted Todd and Beth because they are genuine people—what you see is what you get. And when I got older, I realized how cool they really are (because when I was younger they had to discipline me and stuff if I acted up, easy mistake).

We arrived in Green Bay at a time that every little kid dreads. When autumn comes, things fall apart for kids. In one word: school. We again searched for a new school. I had been to two different schools before second grade, and while that's not any kind of record, it has to be quite shocking to some people. Mom found Bay City Baptist because of its A-Beka-Books curriculum, the same one we used in New Jersey and Tennessee. My sister and I were already up to speed in our subjects; our only adjustment was to go to a Baptist school when we were non-denominational.

In my class there were about 15 people total in the classroom, but in my second grade, there were only two others: Brian and James. My teacher was really cool. But I remember sitting at my table, feeling like the other kids knew who I was, even though they weren't even looking at me. I knew my dad was a big deal in Green Bay, and I hadn't seen very many black people around. That's pretty good reasoning for a second grader. I wasn't wearing or carrying anything that would give me away. But fidgeting in my seat, scratching my pencil with my fingernail, I worried about people finding out "who I am." I was self-conscious whether people knew about me or not. I did not want that extra attention, even in second grade. If I was going to get friends I wanted it to be because of me, not because my dad brought home gobs of money, while recording 120-some sacks in the NFL.

One third-grade kid named Thomas approached me about the second or third day of school and asked me, "Are you Reggie White's son?" I couldn't figure out how people knew. I just told him the truth, but I didn't offer more on the subject. The smile on his face suggested he had just won a prize. Later that week, a new question followed, "How much does your dad make?" At seven years old, I was unaware of just how much money my father was making. And I didn't care. As long as I wasn't being spoiled I didn't care how much money we made, it was all in how I acted. The way I see it, people can act like total snobs and not have anything, others pretend to have it all, and others still don't let their money change them. One's identity lies in actions, not possessions.

But the question of my dad's salary intrigued me, and I went home and asked, "Hey Dad, some kids at school wanna know how much money we make." He didn't waste any time when he said, "You don't make nothing, but as for me, go back and tell the kids at school, 'It ain't none of yo' business.'" Being the obedient child I was, I went back to school and, at recess, told the boy in my best Reggie-growl, "It ain't none of yo' business." A classic good-times moment, indeed. For years my dad would tell that story to everyone; he loved it. That day I learned that our family's business is our own. What is said at home would always be confidential unless otherwise noted. As I got older, I learned what I could or shouldn't say, but I was overly cautious at a young age not to spread around my family's concerns.

From then on, I started to become acquainted with the people in my small school of 75 students. Some of my third-grade friends I would recall forever: Jeremy Schmit, Derek O'Dell, Nathan Ness, and Adam Ness. I was probably closer to Jeremy than any of them. But because all of us were friends, we made so many memories together, all of us could have a good time, and no one felt left out. We had many sleepovers in my basement. We lived to play any number of games, but we really enjoyed connecting to play *NBA Live*. Jeremy and Nathan and another guy were the Bulls, and Derek, Adam, and I were another random team. At that time, Michael Jordan owned his name, which meant that no one could play as him on any type of NBA game. The creators came up with a character called, "Number 89." Everyone knew that was Michael, but while it didn't look like him at all, it sure did play like him. Jeremy would get all psyched out because they, as the Bulls, would demolish us. The way I saw it, anyone could be good with the Bulls—well, the Bulls of that era. But we used to play games all night. Usually we wound up staying up really late, but really I wanted to go to bed. I could play video games anytime. I wanted to sleep. But the other guys wanted to stay up all night, which is understandable. Being the momma's boy I am, I snuck upstairs and crawled into bed with Mom while the rest probably stayed up really no more than an hour. There was room in my mom's bed because during football season, Dad wasn't home on Saturday nights. Even if the Sunday game was at home, the players reported to the hotel Saturday night at 7 p.m. for dinner, planning, and guaranteed rest. But every time I would wake up the next morning, it never failed, Derek was always there to say something like, "We stayed up till six o'clock; you shoulda been there!" Jeremy would do this, Nathan would say that. It was always a blast. Then they'd rag on my choice to go upstairs to sleep with my mom. By that time, I was happy to have everyone out of the house because I had missed all the fun and didn't want to hear about it.

Another time we all slept at Derek's house to play all-night *Nintendo 64*. We were sidetracked by horror movies that Jeremy and Nathan videoed, using fake blood. The poor acting was the best part. Bad camera shots and the worst attempts to look like real blood entertained us. That night was my chance to redeem myself: to sleep downstairs with the rest of them. While I was playing a game on Derek's N64, the room went quiet around me: they had all fallen asleep. I celebrated. I had finally stayed up later than they had. The sun came up on Saturday morning, and I treated myself to cartoons that I watched every Saturday morning. I trotted into the living room, but by this time, I had been up for 22 hours straight. Even though my parents were fine with PG cartoons, Derek's mom said, "Jeremy, they said 'parental guidance.' I don't think you should watch that show." I was mad, fueled, no doubt, because of my sleep deficit; but I was too tired to be crazed. I just fell asleep on the little pillow in the living room floor. Mrs. O'Dell quickly shuffled me out. "Jeremy, don't sleep out here, go in Derek's bed." The next thing I remembered was waking up with a room full of guys saying, "Why is Jeremy in Derek's bed?!" and Derek saying, "Ew, he's drooling on my pillow." At least I had made it all night.

Also, Jeremy is solely responsible for turning me on to cartoons: *Calvin and Hobbes* and *Garfield.* He introduced me to plastic covers to keep the books fresh and new. I was so into *Garfield* that I could almost tell you what comic was in what book just by reading the story line. I even understood many jokes when I was little. Today they are more enjoyable because I do have a deeper understanding. I even have the newspaper comic sent to my e-mail every day.

Occasionally, I went outside to play catch with my dad, but it was more like playing throw with him, because I stopped trying to catch anything he threw. He threw the ball so hard it felt like it would penetrate my body if I let it touch me. It was so hard and fast. I thought if I didn't give it back he couldn't throw it back, either. One night, Dad tucked the Nerf football into bed with me to teach me not to be afraid.

While Dad was acclimating me to the football, he was busy acclimating the Packers to winning. There is a lot of speculation as to how the Lambeau Leap came into existence. I understand that it was popularized by Robert Brooks, but I must say that he was not the first one to do it. In fact, my dad had a lot to do with it, and I never knew that until I was about 16 years old. This is the story. Not only was it the coldest game my dad ever played in in his entire career with below-zero temperatures with the wind chill on December 26,

1993, but it was the day my dad helped out with the Lambeau Leap against the then-Los Angeles Raiders. My dad had picked up a fumble and started to run with the ball when he was about to be driven out of bounds; he lateraled the ball to Leroy Butler just in time, and Leroy caught it and took it 25 yards for what would be the Packers' third touchdown. He then leaped into the stands, starting the tradition. They would ultimately win the game 28-0, and go to the playoffs for the first time in 11 years.

Undoubtedly, my dad liked to voice his opinion, and it was mostly on the news. But one time in his life he was more in the news than he wanted to be. Our church back in Tennessee had burned down. Dad's questioning nature, the one that would spur his learning about the Bible later, was focused on the media. He was mad that it took his own church in Tennessee to be burned down for the news to report that other inner-city churches were burned. Looking at the newspaper, he shook it and said, "Why are they just now reporting on all of these church burnings when they have been happening for years! Why?! Because Reggie White's church burned? It's news now?"

I knew his frustration was that the news didn't necessarily care what happens in the inner city. Columbine was such a big deal because suburban kids weren't normally involved in shootings. Inner-city schools had been getting shot up for years, but no one cared. The biggest problem my dad had with the media is that they only focused on people who had money. He wasn't saying that what happened at Columbine wasn't horrible, but that other places should get news time too, so that they could help prevent that from happening again. The more aware the public is, the better prepared it can be.

From August 1994 to January 1995, our cousins from my dad's side, Khalil and Syiedah, lived with us. Their mother had died, and my parents wanted to help. My sister and I were much younger than they were; Khalil had been in the seventh grade and Syiedah was just beginning high school. Their first night with us, Khalil asked me what time we went to bed, knowing we had to be in bed early because school was the next morning. I told him 7:30. He exclaimed, "7:30!? I thought it would be at least 9:00!" Instantly, he decided this was not going to be a good arrangement. Things only got worse from there for Khalil. He was placed in the seventh grade, and the teacher noticed he could not complete the work. They determined he needed to move back to fifth grade in some subjects and sixth grade in others. That was hard enough on him, but then he realized he would be in my class. Jeremy Schmit and Khalil became good friends. I wasn't so much jealous as I wanted to be included. We still had good times, though; Jeremy and the other guys came over all the time, and we all hung out together. Khalil had thought it was downhill from there, but he came to find that he enjoyed Green Bay more than he thought he would.

One night closer to winter, it was going to start snowing, and I had gone to bed already. Khalil came into the room, turned on the lights, woke me up, and asked, "Hey, Jeremy. Jeremy, wake up. It's morning. Jeremy!"

"What, Khalil?" I was fully awake. My heart was pounding.

"Can we throw snowballs at school?" *I must be dreaming.*

"You woke me up to ask me that?!" It was that kind of waking one does when some facts seem like part of a dream sequence, and one wakes up in mid-sentence.

"Can we?"

I crawled out of my covers and down the hall into my parents' bed to go to sleep. My mom came in and asked, "What are you doing in my bed?"

"Khalil woke me up, but don't tell Dad. I don't want him knowing, 'cause I don't want Khalil getting mad at me." I tried to snuggle down in the sheets.

"Oh, we have to tell him." Mom had insistence in her voice that I dreaded.

"No," I pleaded.

"No, we are telling him; come downstairs with me." She took me by the hand, dragging me. No way did I want to tell on Khalil.

When we got downstairs, I interrupted Dad watching *Law & Order* to tell on Khalil with Mom's prompting finger in my back. I told him I was scared Khalil was going to be mad at me (after all, he was three years older than I). My dad told me that I would be fine in my own bed. Meanwhile, my mom had snuck away because I could hear her upstairs yelling at Khalil, "Don't you know if you wake him up he won't be able to go back to sleep? You have to go to school tomorrow. You don't go waking him up. What were you thinking?" I crept back in my room, feeling like a fink, and tried to sleep. Khalil was mad, breathing hard; but only for that one night.

Syiedah was and still is cool. But now, I understand why she was so easily irritated with my sister and me at times. Syiedah was 14 and Jecolia was seven. That was a huge difference between girls. Barbies and lipstick. Even the music was different. At semester break, Syiedah got a Ricochet, the remote-controlled car that could be controlled even if it turned over. It was the season's fad, and everyone wanted one, and she got one for good grades on her report card. Christmas was days away, and Aunt Valerie (my mom's best friend) sent my sister and me each one. She sent me the blue one and my sister the red. I took that as a mistake and immediately begged Jecolia for the red one. She let me take it. Outside, Syiedah's and Jecolia's cars were crossing frequencies because they were the same ones. I, however, had no problem because I had the only red one. Syiedah yelled at Jecolia, who promptly went inside, and I just kept playing. Years later, I thought back and realized that Jecolia had done nothing wrong. Choosing to be nice to me caused stress for Syiedah, and I felt bad.

There were certain phrases that Syiedah and Khalil said when they came to Green Bay that my sister and I caught onto because we were young and eager to be hip. One of those phrases was, "That's Phat!" The first time my sister and I heard this, we started laughing, "Fat!?" When they explained that it was similar to "cool" and there was a "P-H" where the "F" was supposed to be, all of a sudden it didn't seem so stupid. My sister and I used that phrase about clothes, television, music, each other. Everything we discussed was adorned with the new adjective. That didn't bother them too much.

But one day after school, we were in the van going home and I said, "That's fresh." I had heard Syiedah say that before. She whipped her head around and asked, "Jeremy, did you say that because I did?" I played it nine-year-old cool and told her I had heard it before, meaning I had heard it probably once or twice from Khalil. I decided not to make that phrase a part of my vocabulary. That proved to be good, quick thinking, because our mockingbird style was getting on her nerves; I probably would have reacted similarly if I were in her place.

In gym class, Khalil got on Jeremy's team, but I wanted to be on Khalil's team. I needed him to think I was cool. He asked if I was sad because I wasn't on his team and rolled his eyes when I said yes. He didn't want me to be everywhere with him, and he couldn't understand why I was trying so hard to look up to him. I understand that a lot more now that I am older. The whole concept of having someone like your little cousin or little sibling always wanting to be around you can be annoying.

At school, there was this game that Brian, James, and I used to play. We would all pick a power (like ice, water, or fire), and say it was our power. So I was Fire Man. And I was acting like I had fire powers, able to shoot it out of my body, all cool-looking. At lunch one day, Khalil asked me what kind of superhero I was. I told him I was Fire Man. He and his friends started laughing. He asked, "Did you go around squirting people with your hose?" The whole table was in an uproar, and I said, "No, I mean an actual man of fire." The boys stopped laughing. They had been wrong. And a third grader proved it. That was my first encounter making people shut up about something they knew nothing about. It felt good, because I shut up every last one of the fifth and sixth graders. That was pretty satisfying for me.

Khalil and Syiedah did not stay with us past January 1995. Instead they went back to Tennessee, and I really never saw them too much after that. Sadly, in 2002, at only 18 years old, Khalil was shot inside his own house, interrupting a robbery. He was killed instantly.

My fifth grade teacher really loved the Packers (like most people in the city), and she often incorporated football statistics in her math lessons. For her birthday, the class pitched in, with a hookup through my mom, to buy her and her husband two tickets to the Packers game against the 49ers. When we presented her with the tickets, she went looney. She was screaming and yelling, and she even cried. Remember, in Green Bay fans can't just walk up to the stadium and purchase seats.

Many people have their conjectures about how many Packers tickets we, the White family, were given and for how long. The truth is the Packers gave our family two free tickets—not box seats, not club seats, not side-line passes, not VIP. Two tickets. We did have the option of buying more tickets, but we only got two tickets for free. And no, we did not receive free tickets every week after my father retired from the game. We would get two tickets every week, and my mom would pay extra to have them upgraded to club seats when it was colder. Club seats aren't box seats, but they definitely weren't outside. And my mom always bought two more tickets. Because my sister wouldn't go to a game unless Ed Van Boxtel, owner of several car dealerships in the wider Green Bay area, would invite us into his box, it was always my mom and me. And if friends or family came into town, sometimes they would come with us to the games, or sometimes I could invite two of my friends. Contrary to popular belief, I have only been to two away games in my whole life. One was the Vikings against the Packers at the Dome, and the other was at Atlanta when Dad played with the Carolina Panthers.

The games at Lambeau Field are far from normal. It was always loud, always. The Green Bay fans are probably some of the most loyal, non-bandwagon, "for their team" fans in the whole entire world. Unlike fans who are just fans because the team wins a lot, Packers fans are loyal through thick and thin. That was most evident early on before we won the Superbowl and were not that good of a team. There isn't a stadium on earth like the one in Green Bay. If something great happens, you can hear the fans cheering from miles down the road. The stadium is the centerpiece of the city. Everyone loves the Packers. It's a good place to bring your kids, and the feeling you get at a Packers game is unlike anything else, especially when we win. People are on a waiting list for tickets that they will not get for another 15 years. But to be able to go to one Packers game is worth a lifetime of memories. It's that good. My dad said after they won the Super Bowl in the 1996-1997 season that Packers fans were the best fans on earth, and he wished he could give them all Super Bowl rings. Later, when he would hear players stating that their fans were the best, like Kurt Warner when the Rams won the Super Bowl a few years later, my dad would always say, "Naw, they aren't the best fans in the world at all. Green Bay fans are for real." Nothing against Kurt Warner or the Rams fans, but I still hold true that my dad was right. There's nothing like a Packers fan.

When I was ten, though, I hated to see the fans coming. The worst places seemed to be when we were on vacation. I guess in Green Bay, and later, in Cornelius, North Carolina, people grew accustomed to seeing Reggie White squeezing the produce at Harris Teeter or ordering his favorite ribs and wings at Tony Roma's; but when we were on vacation it was different. When a fan realized he had touched down in the same airport in the same part of the world at the same moment as Reggie White, he suddenly felt entitled to address him. Disney World was the worst. Fans would snap photos of Dad even when he would put up his hands and ask them not to. They were relentless.

Football fans all over the country will recognize the names Ahman Green or Rod Garner, but would they recognize either one of them sitting poolside at a sunny resort? No, unless the fan is a die-hard Packers fan (and what other kind of Packers fan is there?). These popular names are hidden behind football helmets; their anonymity is probable. But the same does not go for the Minister of Defense. Much of the time, Dad would hang back in the hotel room or take the tram back a few hours early to avoid putting us through it. I hear Jake Delhomme of the Carolina Panthers does the same thing; when his wife needs to run into the mall for something, he'll wait in the car. That's a shame.

I always loved to be able to fall asleep on our long plane rides to Ohio—even though I was getting bigger, my dad still liked to show me that he still loved me.

Another interesting thing in fifth grade: I got arrested. It was bound to happen; I lived in a town full of Packers "America's team" fans. One of the greatest defensive linemen to have ever played on the Packers team, and his son rooted for America's team, all right, but not the Packers. I got arrested at school for being a Cowboys fan! The policeman, the father of a boy in my class, put me in handcuffs, told me why he was arresting me, and walked me out the door like I was really going somewhere.

I kept asking, "This is a joke, right? C'mon, this is a joke, right?"

"No, no joke. You *are* a Cowboys fan, are you not?"

"Yeah, but that's not against..." I was beginning to think I was really in trouble.

"Come with me." He tugged at my arm.

In the end it was a joke, thank God. I am still a Cowboys fan, and I still have not been thrown out of my house. My dad had always threatened to burn the Emmitt Smith jersey (that he bought me) and any other Cowboys gear that I had.

I've endured a lot of talk about being a Cowboys fan, but, of course, I was still a fan of my father's team. It was truly a blessing that my dad's ego wasn't so big that he couldn't handle my devotion to Jimmy Johnson. No one could live in Green Bay and not be attached to the Packers; I can't drive that point home enough. It is not possible. The year we went on to win the Super Bowl, we played Carolina in the NFC Championship and crushed them. When we won, my mom was extremely happy; her partner, her soulmate, her love was finally getting a chance to live what he wanted for so long—to actually go to the Super Bowl (he wanted to win it, obviously, but getting there was half the fun). I kept asking her, "What now?" as if she could know. It was a joyful moment in the tiny town, because not only was the team going to the Super Bowl, the whole town was invigorated for the next two weeks leading up to the big game. I remember going into the locker room, ten years old with my clean cut and my three parts in my head, yelling, "Dad we're going to the Super Bowl, we're going to the Super Bowl!"

He looked me dead in the eye and chuckled, "Son. What? You ain't goin' nowhere; you're a Cowboys fan, remember? Ask Emmitt to take you."

I told him, "Aww, Dad, stop, we get to go to the Super Bowl!"

"You think I'm kidding, I'm not kidding." He turned and found teammate Sean Jones. "Sean, Jeremy thinks he's goin' to the Super Bowl. Tell him Cowboys fans can't go to the Super Bowl."

Nodding, Mr. Jones said, "Yeah, you can't be a Cowboys fan and go to the Super Bowl." But then he said, "You know your dad is just playin'." I knew. Dad loved to tell that story on me. My dad loved to pick on me about the Cowboys after he found out how I really perceived him. Every matchup with Dallas before they went to the Super Bowl (save the NFC championship game a year before) I would always tell my dad that the Cowboys were going to whoop up on the Packers. He would always say, "That's what you think." But one day I said it, and it really bugged him. He said, "Jeremy, why can't you root for your dad; why do you have to be a Cowboys fan?" I told him, "Dad, to me you are just Dad; you aren't Reggie White, the great Packers defensive end. You are just Dad." From that point on, he didn't care at all that I was a Cowboys fan. He knew I loved him as just Dad, not for what he did for a living.

It was a Tuesday. Jecolia and I were excited to have Dad pick us up from school, and Tuesdays were his only day off. When we jumped into the car that day, we discovered another of Dad's habits. Stuffed between the console and his seat was a large Burger King bag, and the car still smelled of French fries and every condiment and topping on a hamburger. The soda was only half full. Jecolia and I sensed the awkwardness, and we just looked at Dad. Stared at him, really. He looked at each of us and then put the car in gear. "Don't tell your mama," he said, almost to the steering wheel. We weren't about to give him up to Mom. This went on for years, in Philadelphia and Green Bay; only the bag changed. Of course Mom knew all along. A woman knows when a smell on her man is not her own. And whether it was Burger King or Wendy's, as long as he ate her meal every day at the family table, she didn't complain. But my sister and I thought we had something on Dad.

The next couple of weeks were great. In the back of my mind I knew I was going to take some time off from school and to boot, I was going to the Super Bowl. The flight there was memorable only because all the team's families were flying to Louisiana for Super Bowl XXXI. I really don't remember what I did in Louisiana other than play my cousin's Sega Saturn and stay in the hotel room.

Finally, the day of the big game came. I asked my mom, "You think if I ever decide to play football and go to the Super Bowl that I'll win on my first time too?" She said she didn't know. She probably had an inkling that my talent would not be football. And she was preoccupied. I'm sure she was nervous for my dad. But I knew the whole time we were going to win the game; it was just a matter of letting three hours go by, it's jsut that simple. I did not feel intimidated by the Patriots, and I knew my dad was finally going to get the one thing besides God that he had been wanting all of his life: a Super Bowl ring. He was finally going to be happy in a complete sense of the word.

The game was filled with ups and downs and minor setbacks. Three Patriots fans in front of us kept trying to get me to at least give them a high-five when the Patriots scored, and I wasn't having any of it. Why would I high-five the enemy?

I know some football fanatics are probably wondering what it felt like when my dad got his first of three sacks on Bledsoe in the game. To tell the truth, I missed the first one, and then I looked up and he got another one just like that. And in all honesty, I do not remember the third one. All I knew was that it was crazy and loud in the stadium, and those moments would go down in history. When the game was nearly over, I knew there was not going to be any last-minute comeback; the Packers were going to win Super Bowl XXXI. I went down on the field with Sean Jones, and he brought me to the podium where my dad, Brett Favre, and a couple other players were being interviewed. I remember touching the Super Bowl trophy; it was marvelous. And if you look in the photo close enough you can see me in the back mesmerized by the Super Bowl trophy. The photo is on the Internet, forever archived; the only problem is one of my eyes was closed, sadness.

When they asked my dad about winning the game he gave all honor and glory to Jesus Christ. Everyone was screaming. I remember being very surprised he didn't tell them to be quiet because he sounded like he was going to literally be the "Minister" who had just finished playing "defense." Afterward my dad carried the Super Bowl trophy around the field. Leroy Butler took me back with him while my dad finished an interview with John Madden, once the field cleared out and everyone was gone. Being on the very field where the Packers had brought home a title that they hadn't held in so long was amazing. Just the sheer size of the Superdome in New Orleans had astounded me.

While I was on the field, another scene was going on in the stands with my family and a few others. My mom and our family were sitting in the stands waiting for my dad to go back to the hotel together. All of a sudden, lumps of cheese dropped onto my family. Some of the cheese was hard, pounding some of my younger cousins on the head. My mom became furious, and she ran upstairs, hopped the fence in one leap, showing she was still from the 'hood of Cleveland, and burst in the suite door. She saw all the men drunk and terrified that a woman had just burst in with such a ruckus. The Patriot fans were mad about their loss, and they knew the people below, my family, were Packers fans. She snarled at those men who were bunched up in the corner, scared for their well-being. She raised her finger to them and said, "We have children down there you are hitting with this cheese! You need to take yourselves and do something besides throwing cheese at little children! And get a grip, you drunkards!" Later, my dad would hear that story and, like with similar stories, not be surprised. After all, he had known this woman for a long time, and he knew she would take charge when she needed to.

Funny little tidbit. During the game the film crew showed Reggie White's "wife." Actually, they showed my Aunt Maria on the television around the nation, declaring she was my mom. My mom and my aunt do look a lot alike, but it was funny because Aunt Maria had called in for a few "sick days" to go to the Super Bowl. Of course, some of the faculty saw her on television, and when she came back home, they said, "It's OK. We know your secret: you took a few sick days off to go watch your husband's game."

Off-season for my dad was only a little different. He spent six hours a day running, lifting, and running again to keep in shape. He felt that staying in physical condition year-round helped him be the best player he could be. And it couldn't hurt getting him to another Super Bowl. Dad only brought his A-game in anything he did. Instead of taking a few months off, he was out the door each morning, staying prepared for football season. It amazes me to think what half of the players in the NFL would be today if they had his work ethic.

In sixth grade, I switched from Bay City Baptist to Green Bay Christian. Bay City Baptist was incorporating some changes that my family didn't necessarily agree with. The school felt that the families shouldn't support Hollywood. More often that not, smut was in the foreground. One parent had taken her own son to the movies over the weekend; and the principal called her in to suggest if she were going to continue to go to the movies, do it in the summer, not during the school year. When we were asked to sign a contract promising not to go to the movies, we knew it was time to part ways.

Of course I tried to keep it on the low that my dad was Reggie White. Trying to be a normal kid with a normal experience at a school didn't last long. There are hardly any black people in Green Bay, Wisconsin. Every time one sees a black person one thinks that he plays for the Packers or is related to someone who plays for the Packers. Now, narrow it down to Green Bay Christian. In elementary, there was my sister and two younger black girls; and I was in middle school. I was one of four black people in the entire 300-person private school, and my last name is White. Not a puzzle. Not even a few hours had passed before everyone knew who I was. One kid told me when he first heard about me everyone kept talking about this "white" kid, but when he saw me and I was black, he was confused. Then it clicked.

Yeah, so I should have known, but I always tried to remain Jeremy, not Reggie White's son.

Sitting stiffly in the unforgiving seat in my first class, Bible, I was scared of this new school, bigger than any other I had ever attended; and I was certain this time everyone knew who I was, in regard to my bloodline. The teacher stood and said, "Welcome. This is Bible class. My name is Mr. Mindell. You can call me Mr. Mindell, Coach, or you can even call me "Sports guy." Don't hesitate, just go ahead and yell, 'Hey Sports Guy!'" He put me at ease. Immediately my anxiety receded.

I started to make friends. One girl, Rachel Harris and I became close. We planned to go to the movies with our other classmates. Our first plan was to see *Titanic*. I had no desire to see this movie until all the hype died down. Everyone kept telling me how good it was, but still, I didn't want to see it. We got a ton of people (i.e., ten) to see this movie. This was a big moment for me in my social life because, for the first time, Mom left me alone in public with my friends and someone else's parents. Other than school functions, this is not how my mom let things go down. I felt grown; it was great. During the movie Rachel made me switch with another girl. Later, I found out it was because I was talking too much during the film. What can I say, I've got a knack for talking, but I have gotten better, trust me.

Meeting one guy in particular impacted the rest of my life. His name is Joseph Pierre. When I first asked him his name he nodded and said, "Ay, my name's Joe." I thought he said that his name was Job. C'mon, in my house that's understandable.

Early in the year I became great friends with Joe. The first time he came to my house was after school after our class trip to the skating rink. I was into roller blades, not regular skates. Leaving the rink Joe kept asking, "Jeremy, are you sure it's OK if I come to your house?" I told him it was fine, but he kept asking, "Are you sure? Are you sure?" I told him, "Yes, Joe, yes!" Later, I found out that because he had never heard my mom say it was OK he wasn't sure. He was still asking for reassurance as we jumped into my mom's car. It's Joe.

All of our classmates at Green Bay Christian were close for the most part; we were all a big, maybe not always happy, but a big family. The only time I got in trouble was early on. We would go across the street to a soccer field for gym class. It goes without saying that it's tough enough to get a few kids across a street, but imagine 30. When we crossed the street, my sixth-grade mind thought it would be funny to hide behind the wall and not cross with the rest of the class. Joe looked at me as if to say, "You're really not coming? OK, you'll see what happens." Once everyone else was on the other side, Mr. Mindell yelled, "Jeremy, get over here!" Having to go over by myself was no big deal to me, but the teacher who was responsible for everyone didn't share my sentiment. At the end of the day, I was called to the principal's office. I had received a pink slip. I apologized, and I think I started crying. After that, he prayed with me and another pink-slipped boy from my class. I didn't realize how good the talk and the prayer was until now. My dad always did the same thing. He would remind us that he wasn't some sort of tyrant, but that he loved us; and there was a reason for why he whooped us. Praying with us was the principal's way of telling us that even though he had to discipline us, he still cared.

Going home I didn't know what to expect. Anyone who has parents that discipline them well (and hard) knows the fear of waiting to hear just which punishment is coming. Will it be the grounding, the stiff lecture, or the old standard whoopin'? But when I walked slowly in the front door, hunched over slightly in fear and anticipation, my dad came around his desk and sat down with me on the couch. I had his full attention. Anyone who's lined up against him on Sundays knows that is a little daunting. He calmly asked why I wouldn't just cross the street. Then he said the unbelievable, "I'm not going to give you a whooping now, but if you get another pink slip I will." My heart was pounding in my ears. Did I hear him right? I took this to mean that if I ever got another pink slip I would get a whooping. I felt off the hook, because I knew I wasn't going to get another one.

Sixth grade also would be the year I first had an infatuation. There was this really pretty girl named Charissa. From the first day I saw her, I liked her. I couldn't stop looking at her. But there was something about her I knew that even if we did become boyfriend and girlfriend (in sixth grade…wow) that it wouldn't work, and that it wouldn't be beneficial to me. Later, (and I'll spare the details here) I came to figure out that I was right, but my infatuation remained.

Aside from all my girl problems, there were also sports problems. It wasn't like I got cut from the team and my dreams of becoming a basketball star were ruined, quite the opposite. I played soccer, then I made the team. I was with a good group of guys; but, goodness gracious, we were terrible! We could not win a game. Throughout sixth grade, I was either the post player or the wing player, so one might think I was a big guy and could stop anyone in the paint. Well, one would be wrong. And for the thought, *Hey, Jeremy is black, so he must have been good, strike two. But, at least Jeremy had a lot of white guys on his team who could shoot well.* Then, as they say in base-ball, you're out. Our team stunk. Our team was no good, no talent, no skill, no direction, nothing. We knew the game of basketball, but we couldn't play it. We all loved game day, but we dreaded what happened at the end: we lost. We just weren't any good. But that didn't keep us from having fun. Oh no. The only person frustrated on our team was the coach. It wasn't just that we were losing, but sometimes we didn't practice seriously. Go figure.

It is most important to have fun in sports, because if one is not having fun, then what good is a win? Even if my dad had not want-ed to step out onto the field every time he did, he always tried to have fun. One could see it in his eyes in practice, after a sack in a game, even on the sideline when his teammate did something well. Too many parents push their kids to play sports not because they want their kids to have fun or be part of a team, but because the parents have this obsession with living their own sports dreams through their children. Parents who do that, please stop. Just because a nine-year-old on a school soccer team loses a game or misses a goal that he "should have made" does not mean that he is a failure in life or that he should be yelled at. Yelling is not encourage-ment. They are kids. Children. Yelling to a kid is yelling; the words are irrelevant. And parents who didn't get the chance to be super-stars themselves don't get to re-create themselves through their children. Fumbling the ball in a Pop Warner football game will not destroy the boy's career any more than making a touchdown will begin it. Not once did my father ever force me to play or not play any sport. He wanted me to pursue my own dreams; my aspirations were his goal for me. I am so thankful he never forced me to do anything toward a specific profession in life. He went after what he was good at and wanted, and he knew it was important to let me do the same.

In our spare time, and some of us made time, kids went to 180, a Christian youth group that was part of the church we attended. On Wednesday nights, 180 was the place to be. There was indoor basketball, a little concession area, video games on a big-screen television; it was just a nice hangout for youth. Did I mention the video games? I scrambled to get there practically every Wednesday. It was my home away from home because all my friends went, and I craved being with everyone, hanging out and talking about God. Joe introduced me to 180 because it was fun, clean, and real. We had contests during the service and little skits during youth group. It was entertaining and teaching us a message. Pastor Karl was a great guy, and everyone loved him. He was so real and could be on one's level at any point in time.

Being involved in 180 was partially a conflict of interest between my parents and me. They didn't mind that I went to 180, but they were conflicted with the church from which the youth group stemmed. The church had used my dad. They used his name and status to build their church. When I say "build their church," I don't mean to help other Christians and non-Christians. I mean they used my dad to draw people to their church for money. Being used and manipulated for a man to reap financial benefits wasn't entirely new to my parents; but usually Mom would get a vibe from people and avoid the situation altogether. But she isn't perfect. Later, the pastor told Dad directly to his face (once we were living in North Carolina) that he did, indeed, use my dad. My dad had felt uneasy and asked the pastor outright if he used his status to build the church, and the pastor said yes.

Another reason behind my parents' unrest about the church dealt specifically with me. In one service, a guy from out of town, let's call him Sim Tory, was a "healer." Since my family and I were grounded on faith, I went up to get my ear prayed for. Before I did, Sim told a story about how he had heard a minister who was called to Africa to perform healing. The people who were touched with the Holy Spirit could not get off the ground for three hours because the Holy Spirit was so strong in them. As I walked up to be prayed for, Sim pushed me back, I fell, and I lay there, hoping to be healed of my deafness in my left ear. Lying there, I wondered if I would be able to move for three hours just like the people in Africa. An usher came up to me and said softly into my right ear, "Sim wants you to stay on the ground; don't get up." At that time I thought that maybe he did not want me to be a distraction as he was giving his closing statements. I could understand that. Later that week, I told my parents what had happened. They couldn't believe it. The biggest problem my dad had with "healers" is that they give themselves all the credit and aren't humble. "Healers" in the Bible always said that their power was not their own, but God's. I do not recall Sim ever saying God worked through him. The whole event was about Sim Tory, Sim Tory, Sim Tory. More evidence that he was trying to uplift himself was his re-creation of people not being able to get off the ground by having me stay on the ground. It's really a shame.

What my dad believed concerning healing was even more radical when we moved to North Carolina, and he started studying. He found that in the Bible God would send false prophets amongst his people. And these false prophets would perform wonders and mar-velous things, but do not follow these people because they are not of Him. God would send these people to test us so that He may know who is serving Him or not. The Sim Tory story was a great example. That wasn't a service to promote God, that was a service to promote man. Because immediately after when I tried to tell him I thought my ear was healed, he gave me a dismissive gesture and just scooted past me to meet my father. He didn't care about me; he cared about his status.

About my ear, I am healed. I can't hear out of it at all, but I am healed. The doctor told my parents, when they discovered the hearing loss, that I would not be able to walk steadily, play organized sports, or do anything that required my equilibrium to be stable. However, my equilibrium is just fine. When God told my parents He would heal my ear, He did. Although my parents first interpreted that to mean I would one day be able to hear, that's not what He meant. I can function nearly perfectly; and often, people don't believe that I'm completely deaf in one ear.

One day, six months after I had started Green Bay Christian, Rachel Harris and I were talking on the phone, because good friends have a lot to talk about: our workload, people in school who were mean to us, just life in general. When we talked about family, she said, "Jeremy, I need to tell you something important. In the beginning of the year, I heard you were Reggie White's son." I told her it was fine. She said, "Yeah, but the thing is, I wanted to be your friend because of who your dad was. I didn't even know who he was. I just knew he was famous so I started to be your friend for that reason alone. After I got to know you, I stayed your friend because of you, not because of your dad. I just wanted you to know that I am not your friend because of your dad now, but that was why I wanted to be." She asked me if I was mad at her, I told her I wasn't. I really wasn't mad at all. I can't say I knew her initial intentions, but she never exhibited signs of taking advantage of me and my sixth sense never kicked in. When she admitted it, I was just surprised. It just goes to show that even kids in middle school can have agendas. It didn't matter how old I was, I was right for having my guard up, even as far back as a five-year-old. I still question people's first impressions of me. I get paranoid when they don't say that they know I'm Reggie White's son. I always think, *Who knows and who doesn't?* I don't let it change my behavior, but I keep a close eye out for things that I'm not sure about.

At 11 years old, I preached at 180. I spoke on temptation and how we can't blame the devil for our temptation, but we must blame our sinful nature. Temptation can come into our lives involving any-thing, and I offered an altar call for those to come forward who wanted to have prayer for the temptation in their lives. In that les-son I knew mostly what I was talking about. When my dad came and said a little tidbit after me, he used one of my lines saying that we can't let Satan tempt us, fall into the temptation, and then have Satan stab us in the back with a worse feeling. The group thought he took that from me, when really, I took it from his many sermons I heard.

My dad was the type of person that couldn't be ridiculed because he always put his own faults out there. When my dad spoke at 180, he addressed God's word, but he also mentioned, in accordance with his subject of that day, that sex stays with you. He said that whomever you have sex with will be connected to you for the rest of your life. The example he gave was from his own experience. He said, "I used to sleep around a lot before I got married. And even to this day when I see someone that looks like a person I had sex with, something in me jumps because I remember." He made the point that a sexual connection can affect you more deeply and cause much regret, and waiting for marriage spares those feelings.

Another time I spoke in sixth grade at a church we attended when we visited North Carolina (before we eventually moved there). I talked about Revelation and how all of the tribulation is going to happen with people who aren't saved by God. Later, I learned I was totally wrong. In one instance I was wrong because I didn't have any business trying to teach on Revelation at 12 years old. On the other hand, my dad would later come to believe and to teach me that even people who believed in God would remain on earth during the tribulation. The rapture would happen after the seven years of tribu-lation. My dad would learn this when I was 15 years old, and after that, the *Left Behind* series sure didn't mean that much to me any-more.

Something entirely new and unexpected happened in sixth grade: my family lived the entire year in Green Bay. We didn't go back to Tennessee after football season. And I was loving every minute of it. I had a great school, a great youth group, and great friends. The only bad part of that year was the Super Bowl.

The 1997-1998 season was going great. We didn't have as good a record as the year before, but we had a game that, to me, was bigger than the Super Bowl: Green Bay Packers versus Dallas Cowboys at Lambeau Field. Every other year we played at Dallas, and we always lost. I always told my dad they were going to lose, and every single time, they did. But this time was different. This time Dallas was coming to play the Packers at home. I knew undoubtedly that the Packers would beat them because the Packers were unstoppable at home and had been for three years running. When Dallas came in, that stadium was so hyped. Troy Aikman was making so many mistakes, and the game was child's play for the Packers as they just ransacked Dallas at every turn. Even though Dallas had a respectable record of 5-5 when they arrived in Green Bay, the Packers won 45-17. In the car after the game, Dad said, "Some of the referees weren't calling some things on us," meaning the Packers had committed a few penalties that the referees "didn't quite see." Even I was happy that the Packers had finally beaten the Cowboys, the team we couldn't quite beat before. At that time, the Packers were becoming known as "America's team" while the Cowboys had held that title for the longest time.

All did not end well. In Superbowl XXXII in sunny San Diego, the Denver Broncos took on the Green Bay Packers. Now I knew we were a good team, and I just knew we would win, just like Superbowl XXXI when we beat the New England Patriots. Unfortunately, Terrell Davis, the Broncos star running back ran all over us. John Elway completed many passes for great gains, and eventually he, himself, ran in for a touchdown. Meanwhile, it was the fourth quarter with just over two minutes to go that I realized we might not win. My cousin Wesley was crying like a baby. I leaned over to him and said, "Anything is possible with Jesus, anything." And a female Packers fan sitting in front of us turned around and told my cousin, "You know, he's right." But at the end of the game we could hear all these cheers. But they weren't ours. The

Broncos had won. They had won the Super Bowl. It was enough to make me stop believing in God. OK, so it wasn't that bad, but I had you for a second, didn't I?

My dad had just lost one of the biggest games of his life because of the Broncos. I didn't care for Terrell Davis or John Elway after that, whatsoever. Every time I hear, "We are the Champions" by Queen, I'm jolted right back to that game, including the sadness and disappointment. Right in my throat. I hated the Broncos, I hated San Diego, I hated everything and I just wanted to leave. I was crying, my cousin was crying; and my mom and aunt, oh, they were laughing. They were laughing about something that had nothing to do with the game. In my 11-year-old mind, I'm thinking, *How can you laugh at a time like this?* Looking back on it, I was as dramatic as if someone had died. To this day I still hate the Broncos. I always root against them, I never play as them on a video game, and I don't watch any highlight reel that shows John Elway diving into the end zone against the Packers defense. Indeed, it took me a good while to get over the fact that we lost. Still stings a little.

Even when we went to the Pro Bowl in Hawaii, I told my dad to make sure he sacked John Elway. He assured me he would try. I remember being on the balcony of our hotel room with a water balloon and seeing John Elway down below. No, no, I didn't do it, but I was tempted. And my mom didn't make it that much better. I told her I wanted to do it, and she just laughed. But in the back of my mind, I knew if I did it, my dad would have pummeled me. Today, I just want Mr. Davis and Mr. Elway to know that I do not despise them the way I used to when I was younger. It was a game, and I'm glad they got theirs. Especially John Elway, man, did he ever deserve it.

That year, when Dad was nominated for Miller Lite Player of the Year he asked to have his name taken off the list. He couldn't accept an award that was sponsored by beer. His principles guided him and directed us. He could have more accolades, more fame, even, if he had won that honor; but Dad couldn't find honor in an alcohol-sponsored award. He taught us through his action every day.

During the break, our family went to Greece to visit Corinth on the "Footsteps of Paul" tour. The tour guide mentioned how they wanted to rebuild some of the desolate historical buildings in the area. I took two rocks about six inches wide to have as a memory of my visit. One of our tour guides grabbed them as I was getting off of the bus at our hotel. He asked, "Are those rocks from Corinth?" I told him they were. He said I should be careful because I was not supposed to take those. I put both of the rocks in my back pocket, and my pants started sagging. I told my mom, and she said, "I'm sure he was kidding." To this day, I don't believe he was, and I jokingly say that I am a fugitive now.

Coming into seventh grade couldn't have been better; Joe and I were close, and I was excited to come back to the school I loved. For the first time I had spent a whole year at *one* school, and this fall, I would not be the new kid. I didn't have to worry about people saying, "Hey are you Reggie White's son?" I found a new pleasure in hearing new kids ask and my "old" friends saying, "Oh, that's so funny! They want to know if you're Reggie White's son. I see how that can get annoying after a while." I was finally in one spot and could call it home.

I wanted to have a girlfriend. I started liking this younger girl (sixth grader) Celeste. When I told another girl in Celeste's class that I liked Celeste, she gave me two days to ask Celeste to be my girlfriend. This was some kind of pressure, I must say. That Friday I had written her a note that told her that someone in my class liked her. Once a month we had "Fun Night" at Green Bay Christian and everyone came to play basketball, volleyball, and other games. There were snacks too. The moment came, and Celeste asked me to reveal her secret admirer. And I calmly and casually pointed to myself with my popsicle. She said, "You?" I nodded my head softly. I could almost hear the violins in the background. For the rest of the night I was shy because she finally knew. I asked her to be my girlfriend, and it lasted. It lasted until three weeks later when she called to break up with me. I cried and cried, but looking back on it I don't know why. Of course I didn't love her. I think I just didn't want to be dumped. Ah, seventh grade.

My mom knew of my secret affair, but my dad had no knowledge of it until about three years later. I'm sure he felt bad being kept out of the loop, but I didn't want to tell him because I wasn't exactly sure how he'd react. When he asked me as a youngster who my girlfriend was, that was harmless because I didn't have hormones; but in seventh grade he couldn't be too careful so he never really asked me if I had a girlfriend. And I wasn't in the habit of telling people, even my mom and dad, who I had liked.

For the first time, I wasn't the new kid. I knew all the inside jokes with the teachers, and I really felt like I was a part of that school. Until now, I was always unaware what would happen at the end of the calendar year (in Jersey and Green Bay) or what had happened at the beginning of the year (in Tennessee).

Soccer season that year was probably the most fun I had playing a sport to date. We only lost two regular-season games. One of the teams we lost to we were able to play again that season. That was also the same Monday night when the Packers played the Vikings. I remember my mom asking me if I was ready to go to the game, and I told her I wasn't ready to go yet because I wanted to see our team win. Up to that point the Packers had won three straight years at home. We were a little late to the Monday Night game because I was waiting to see if we beat the team we had previously lost to. We did. When I realized we won I was so happy that I ran toward the sideline where the game was just finishing up and slid on the wet grass in my pants while pumping both of my arms up and down in the air, screaming. We lost a game in the playoffs, but I only remember it clearly because the same rainy night, the Packers' three-year winning streak at home ended to the Vikings. Randall Cunningham, who had played with my dad in Philadelphia, was the Vikings quarterback. He had a great night. Surprisingly, that game was one of the only times that I saw my dad commit a penalty. He jumped off-sides near the end of the fourth quarter. I could almost feel his frustration.

Seventh grade proved to be a better basketball year. We got a new student named Dan Swan, and he was probably the only one with some decent skill. He could handle the ball. This year we could score, and our family and friends could cheer. But they only got to do that a little in the opening because the score ended at 51-9. Ugh. We had a new coach who kept saying, "Don't worry, guys, it's just the first game of the season." We went on to lose many more games, but one game in particular stands out because we had to drive an hour to play, and they hadn't won a game either. Two teams, neither havibng won a game all season, about to play each other, one team is going away saying, "We won finally!" and the other will leave in ultimate defeat. The words, "We couldn't even beat a team that had never won a game," ringing in their ears.

The game started well, neck and neck. In the final few seconds, down by one, we needed one basket to lead and to hold them off to win the game. It was passed underneath to Joe, and everyone was screaming different things to him, "Pass!" "Shoot!" "Call time out!" He got so distracted with all the confusion that he just jumped into the air with the ball. I could see it in slow motion and hear myself shouting, "Noooooo!" Joe got a whistle for an up-and-down, giving the other team the ball. We lost. It was almost like a curse. God was never going to let me win in organized sports. Before long, I bounced back. That was just the way of the world, and I had to deal with it. Even if I lost, I didn't sulk. I never saw Dad stay mad longer than a few hours. His resilience taught me temperance. For the rest of my time in Green Bay we didn't win another game, but we still had fun.

Another big moment in my family life happened about the same time. My dad spoke at the Wisconsin Legislature. For all the critics, bad mouths, the people who assume, the haters, and the people who just don't want to listen—let me share how things really went down:

My father was asked innumerable times to speak at the Wisconsin State Legislature. Because of his schedule with football and with preaching around the country during the off-season he never had time. In the fall of my seventh grade year, he decided it was time to preach at the Wisconsin State Legislature. The Legislature did not give him a particular topic; they just wanted to hear Reggie White. Contrary to popular belief, they did not give him only five minutes to talk; they told him he could talk for as long as he wanted. Until the day before the speech, he prayed about what to say. As he prayed to God, I remember him pacing the floor in the den, vacillating between topics, and discussing it with my mom. His message was responsibility and synergy. People have to be responsible for their own actions and raise their own children. People have to reach out to others and not be judgmental. Today, to ask the average person (who may or may not have heard it personally) will inaccurately generate the reply, "homosexuality." That may be all people remember about the speech. But thanks to the technology age, anyone curious enough may log on to the Wisconsin Legislature website and access the speech in its entirety. Uncensored and unedited. Interestingly, he only spoke briefly that homosexuality is a sin, according to the Bible. But the media took that statement and turned it into his thesis. At home, he tried to find every possible way to not say "Homosexuality is a sin." He wanted to say, "Sodomy" or "A man lying with another man or a woman lying with another woman." He was trying to find some other word besides "homosexuality." But the night before, he believed he was supposed to make the point to the Legislature that homosexuality was a sin. It is what it is, without softening the edges. And not finding an appropriate euphemism solidified that thought.

Throughout life, if Dad felt that God was calling him to do or say something, he would do or say it without worrying about what everyone else thinks, at all. The only time, and I mean the only time, he would be concerned with what someone else thought was when he confided in someone, and they turned on him. It happened a lot with the so-called "Christians" we had met in our life. But that's something entirely different.

Some might be wondering, "But why? That doesn't make any sense. Why talk to a group of political people about morals?" Maybe he was before his time, because if he were to make that speech today with all the marriage laws that are coming into political question, it would have been more appropriate, and perhaps, more accepted. By some, anyway.

If you ask me, he would have been better off going to a church and preaching about that there are all the atrocities being ignored or allowed within the church that are not labeled as "sins," but more on that later.

During the speech he mentioned that one should love the person but hate the sin, and then he went on to discuss how each individual race has its own unique gifts. It came off as racial stereotyping; but in actuality, he did not intend that at all. I think that was just the icing on the cake for the media because people did not appreciate that he was openly denouncing the homosexual lifestyle. Ironically, after his speech he received a standing ovation, signed a few autographs, and shook some hands. There was no dissension. It wasn't until the next day that all hell broke lose. Some of the very people with whom he shook hands and signed autographs, bad mouthed him less than one day later. Ironically, two lesbians in the audience called my dad personally and apologized for the media, after the media attacked my dad. Journalism is one thing, but lying, demoralizing someone else, and even stretching the facts to make yourself look better is wrong.

I know a lot of people disagreed with him, and they still do. But to the Christians and the believers out there, what he was saying was 100 percent Biblical. If there's one thing my dad always said, one can't believe only part of the Bible. To believe this part, one must believe another part because it is all God's Word. Either be hot or cold, but don't be lukewarm.

But yes, he got pounded for that. We were getting hate mail like crazy, and people were calling him a bigot. He didn't care; he brushed it off. He knew that if he was to believe in God—the God of the Bible—and the Bible itself, then he needed to stand by it word for word. He didn't need to back down. He needed to stand strong on his beliefs, no compromises; and he knew God had his back in the end. And I think that made people scared. There aren't many people who will not compromise because they are too weak to stand against something that isn't "politically correct." Some of the greatest people in history didn't hide in the crowd, but stood out from it. Dad was one of those people who wasn't going to compromise to be politically correct; if he had, then what would he have to live for? We have too many people with beliefs–Christian or not–and they don't know why they believe it.

After he retired, Dad had reached a verbal agreement with CBS to become an in-house color commentator for three years. In a phone conference with Mom, Dad, and Dad's agent, Jimmy Sexton, the president of CBS said he would have to withdraw the offer because of Dad's comments about homosexuality to the Wisconsin Legislature. His reason, he stated, was he was afraid the homosexuals would boycott CBS. When Dad asked what about the Christians, he was told the Christians weren't organized enough to boycott.

Still, I think he would have been better preaching all that in a church. What is the Church itself coming to when they take more pride in telling people to tithe than they do in denouncing certain sins? I am not just talking about making homosexuals leaders in churches. We have thieves, liars, cheaters, adulterers, homosexuals, and some outright bad people leading the church, saying it is acceptable to do things that God finds detestable. And these same men are calling themselves "of God." It baffles me how one has a big church that is more concerned with its profit rather than its pastor who is sleeping around with different women of the church, without regard to his own wife. Or another pastor who gets up in front of his congregation and openly admits he sleeps with other men, that he won't change, and that his congregation will have to decide to remain silent. Whatever happened to us keeping God's commandments? Whatever happened to us as God's people being Holy, which means "Set Apart" in Hebrew? When did we as believers get so scared of other people's perceptions that we are too scared to stand up for our beliefs?

Playoff season, the Packers were paving the road again to the Super Bowl, Super Bowl XXXIII. I knew, I just knew we were going to Miami. Brett Favre made a great play to wide receiver Antonio Freeman who found the end zone for a last-minute score. I figured we had won the game, as there were only two minutes left to play. Little did I realize how strong a quarterback the 49ers had in Steve Young. He led them in an amazing drive toward the goal line. I was hoping and praying they wouldn't complete the drive because if we lost this game, there went my next week in Green Bay. If we lost this game, I would have to leave the one place on earth I wanted to be, Green Bay. Eight seconds left on the clock, Steve Young dropped back to pass and fired one to the end zone. He found none other than Terrell Owens in the end zone. Owens caught it and hung on after getting hit hard by Darren Sharper. When I saw that he caught the ball, tears rolled down my face, and I wailed like a lost baby. Not only did we lose the game, that was the end for my dad in Green Bay, Wisconsin. He was retiring. I remember saying, "Why couldn't someone just put up a hand and block the pass?" I was mad and sad. We should have won that game.

After the first semester of my seventh grade year my dad retired from the game of football. I wondered how his career went so fast. My dad had always talked about "when I retire," but I never thought the future would arrive until it was front and center. He always talked about how he would ride his motorcycle more when he retired and how we were going to travel more (oh, great! Like we didn't travel enough with him preaching everywhere). He said he couldn't wait to just settle down. One would think he was talking about giving up the "fast life" and getting married. But then as quickly as I thought about all those things he wanted to do and probably wouldn't, a harsh reality set in: goodbye, Green Bay. We were never going to live there again. Of all the places we had lived, nothing compared to Green Bay. It held all my childhood moments, good and bad. There, I grew up, learned what it meant to stand for something, and started to become the young man that would make my dad proud. It was the city that got a Super Bowl title and my father was a large part of it. Green Bay is where his dreams came true, too, where he envisioned, "being able to hold the Super Bowl trophy in my hands." Green Bay can't be recreated, and it can't be fully appreciated by outsiders. Green Bay was very accepting of my dad and our family. One of the best parts is that for every 100 white people in Green Bay there is probably only half a black person, but I never felt color barriers at all. Certainly, Green Bay is a one of a kind city.

7

Originally we were supposed to move to Kenosha after Dad's retirement. But all the doors to Kenosha closed. And interestingly, Dad felt like God was calling him to move to Charlotte, North Carolina. All I cared about was our leaving Green Bay. I really didn't mind if we ended up in Alaska, because it hurt too much to be away from the place I loved. My dad finally decided that God indeed wanted him to move to Charlotte.

While our house was being built, I thought for a moment there was hope to stay in Green Bay just a little longer. But alas, no. Since Dad was already retired, we couldn't stay in Green Bay; that would be like dangling raw meat in front of a hungry tiger. Off to Ohio by my mom's family we went.

My mom decided to home school us to ease the transition into a new curriculum in the middle of the year. My mom taught my sister and me for the rest of the school year. The downside, of course, was we didn't get to know anyone because we were at home all the time. The people we lived near were either new families with very young children or retired people with grown children. For practically eight months, my life consisted only of my own family, immediate or otherwise.

Until I entered eighth grade, Dad's religious goals were traditional: be a good person, be able to handle persecution, be respectful representing God and all young black men. Be polite and listen to Mom and Dad. Make sure you read your Bible. And start to immerse yourself into what God wants you to do with your life. This is what I call the "everyday" stuff. It should be understood that in Ohio, Dad was in an infant stage of studying the Bible to learn the history and traditions of the people who lived during that time. There was quite literally more to come.

When Dad retired he missed the guys and being competitive. If he had gone directly into coaching or commentating, he may have made a smoother transition, but just stopping cold turkey was taxing on him. He didn't, however, miss the training or the training camp, but the changeover wasn't difficult only on Dad. My sister and I had to adjust to having him home a lot more than he had been. Not that it was bad to have him home more, but it was similar to having a new babysitter. When parents let their children participate in certain activities, watch some movies, play specific games, but then the babysitter gets there and vetoes the nightly Pokémon competition, and the kids are grouchy. Instead of that 30 minutes of cartoons before bed every Thursday, bedtime becomes 7:30 instead of 8:00. Again, crabby kids. For Jecolia and me (and probably, Mom) it would have been easier if my dad had tempered his retirement with another position. Not having another occupation left all his attention on us.

A lot of alone time gave way to a new interest for me. I became obsessed with Pokémon. I collected the cards, I played the card game, I played the Nintendo games, I watched the show, I knew the Pokerap. Even on my 13th birthday, I got Pokémon gifts and my favorite character was Bulbasaur. I was that into it.

In school, I didn't know how I would do in algebra because in seventh grade at Green Bay Christian, I had pre-Algebra, and Mom moved me straight into Algebra in my home schooled second semester. The book she and I used was the worst, and I never felt that I got a good algebraic experience in middle school.

As school approached, I took my mind off of it by going to Geauga Lake (currently Six Flags Ohio), the day before. I had a good time with my cousin Wesley. I never liked Sundays because school was the next day. At least Sundays before Dad's retirement were better during the season because I could always watch him on television or in person, depending on the game. And if it was a *Monday Night Football* game that was even better because Monday would actually be a fun day of the week. Since he was retired there wasn't going to be any more of that. And the anxiety of being at a new school again gnawed at me. Cuyahoga Valley Christian Academy, CVCA was going to be my new school for a year and a half. Knowing this school was temporary added a new dimension. As soon as I settled in, I would be moving.

While the first week didn't seem so bad, I quickly dreaded going to Algebra. I had already decided to take another year of Algebra because I didn't feel like I understood it well enough to take geometry. If that weren't enough, I got about three hours of homework a night. Many people I've talked to say eighth grade was the hardest year because it was getting them ready for high school, but actual high school was a breeze. So much emphasis was put on homework, I worried about school like never before. Every time I thought I was ahead, I found I was actually behind. Even when I realized I needed to go back to pre-Algebra, I still had too much homework every night. I usually got home from school about 4:00, and if I was finished at 6:00 with my homework, that was a good day. Sometimes my parents would have to make me stop doing homework to come down to dinner. I did homework all the time.

Socially, I had fun at my biggest private school to date. In seventh to 12th grade, there were 700 students. But because Ohio was such a short-lived experience, I can't even tell you first and last names of most of the friends I made in eighth grade. I didn't have time for frivolous relationships, and I wasn't going to lead on anyone.

I met a girl named Adrienne Zeiler. Adrienne is probably the only girl I still keep in touch with from Ohio. She always had questions concerning God, and I listened and gave truthful answers. She was one of the first people to help me in my walk with God in a way I'm sure she was unaware. Her questions about God strengthened my faith and what I knew to be true about God and His Word. She could talk to me about stuff, and I was there for her. My dad was able to do the same thing. People used to call him for advice on any subject, all the time. Many times I heard him on the phone, saying, "Well, if I were in your situation this is what I would do." Then he would explain himself with genuine concern. I find, and with no question Dad taught me, the best way to have someone trust me is to not judge him but to listen and to be their friend. That's what my dad would have wanted me to do with Adrienne and anyone else.

We found a church that would later be called Grace Community Church. Pastor Charles Brewster and his family are wonderful people. Our families were connected in and out of church. We lived near them, and my parents had a mutual love and respect for Chuck and Candy Brewster. We went to church often, and Pastor Brewster spoke mainly from the Old Testament. Most preachers and pastors I had grown up hearing liked to speak more about the New Testament and stayed away from the Old Testament. He liked to talk about the prophets, mainly Isaiah. He and Dad shared a common ground beyond a love of the Lord. They both were studying Hebrew.

As the school year progressed, my dad started changing in a way that the family had never seen before; he started to question the very faith he had been accustomed to for so long. It should be noted, however, that he was not trying to change religion, he was not trying to go against the Bible, and he was not trying to serve another God. He was simply trying to find the truth in the Bible that had been hidden from him, purposely or unconsciously, for so many years by people he had trusted.

He first made this decision on an airplane, coming home from a speaking engagement. Ironically, at the time, I was sitting close, probably just playing some Pokémon on my Gameboy, having a good time, unaware those days were numbered. Dad was reading a book entitled, *Will the Real Heretics Please Stand Up?* by David W. Bercot. When Dad came home, he said that God had spoken to him and asked him,

"Who appointed you to be a preacher, Reggie?" Dad had realized he had been appointed by the man who gave him his preaching license, and that God had never appointed him to preach; therefore, he need not do it until God told him to go out and begin preaching again.

Now for all the critics out there, this is not an open invitation to say, "You see, Reggie believed in a false God all along," or "He never should have said what he said at the Wisconsin Legislature," or "Wait, do you mean that everything he did when he spoke was all for naught and that he didn't help anyone and that he should have never spoken to people in the first place?"

This is not the case, because the God he believed in was the same God he would continue to follow. He had a mandate to say what he said at the Legislature, because it was from God's Word; and finally, even if God didn't tell him to do it, he still helped people. It was not all in vain. Because my father came to the realization that God never appointed him to preach, but that man had, my dad decided immediately to step down from public preaching until God told him it was acceptable to start again. I'm sure many people were disappointed by this, as he was probably on a good number of schedules since he was now retired from football. In the meantime, he felt he had to study God's word to the fullest extent possible to be ready when the call came. This would mean sitting down and digging into what God's word was really about. For hours. Days. Years, if necessary. He didn't know what he was about to get himself into, but it would be a story that all who heard it would never forget.

Because of the hardships at school, my mom felt peace from God in home schooling me for the remainder of the school year starting in January. Even Dad was able to help more with us and spent more time with Mom. He taught me history and religion, and he visited Mom's relatives nearby regularly. Mom and I went back to algebra; and by May, I passed a North Carolina end-of-course algebra exam given by a school to which I would later go. We had family Bible study every Friday night; and 20 people gathered for dinner each week, while Dad would minister for an hour. Then we'd have two to three hours of fellowship, because no one wanted to leave.

This family Bible study was a slow catalyst for my dad's personal desire to study deeply the Bible. Slowly, steadily, and surely, his findings made their way into our home as he began to point out more sins than we originally and commonly thought about. He didn't necessarily find out information that people didn't know, but he brought it to their attention all in a few sermons. Other sins he pointed out were thinking bad upon your fellow man, murder of your fellow man through your thoughts, lusting without actually doing any physical action, and not loving yourself. It wasn't necessarily anything new, he just revisited it in Bible study.

Interestingly, we could always tell when Dad started to learn new things because we'd come home from a day of school or shopping and something would be missing. Certain items started disappearing from our house. Japanese paintings with writing he didn't understand and certain statues that may have represented something long ago and could still be representative today were taken out of our house. The Japanese paintings were thrown out because Dad had read that sometimes curses are put on paintings, and since he didn't know Japanese, he didn't want it in his house. It was too risky to keep it. He always cracked jokes about many young people's fad of Chinese or Japanese tattoos and not really knowing for certain what the markings mean. For all they knew it could truly mean, "I'm stupid."

But the exodus that affected me the most at the time was Pokémon. My dad only really tolerated Pokémon when I started getting into it. I think the amount I had mentally invested in Pokémon annoyed him. It could temporarily take away all the stress in my life. Dad's suspicions about Pokémon's demonic nature drove him to investigate, and he found information he didn't like. He didn't like some of the Psychic Pokémon, the whole Pokémon game in Japan being called "Pocket Monsters" (can't have monsters); and how, inevitably, in his mind, if one of them was bad, all of them were possibly bad.

The Reverend James Dobson made, to my father, at least, a compelling argument against Pokémon. Because it seemed innocuous it must be part of the ploy. That was enough for Dad. Pokémon had to

pack its bags and move out of the White house. I was irritated
because I felt he was thinking closed-mindedly and was taking away
the one thing I enjoyed. I was a 13-year-old boy who was not interested in sneaking out of the house, going to wild parties, taking
drugs, drinking alcohol, or wanting to have sex with anyone. I did-
n't have many friends because I had just been uprooted from my
home and Instant Messenger hadn't been invented yet. I was living
in a temporary house, surrounded by old people; and the only
pleasure I sought and received was from this game. Pokémon was a
way for me to have fun, like boys and their video games, like girls
and their dolls. But now Dad said something I thought was decent
and gratifying was a no go. He wouldn't even let me sell them,
because he didn't want "someone else having evil in his house" if he
didn't agree with it in his. I had over 500 cards (not including the
ones my sister considered "hers") and many rare cards. I could have
made at least $300 off my collection. If it hadn't been just the begin-
ning, I'd swear it was the end of the world.

My parents always say to be careful what you bring into your
spirit. Even your subconscious can take information deep into your
soul. But at 20, I still see Pokémon as a strategic math game. A logic
puzzle. A form of harmless entertainment. But Dad saw it differently.
Mom, Jecolia, and I all were against him in this decision, but it was
his decision. This was the first time in White history that Dad actually got mad at the three of us for "coming against him" at the same
time. I figured it was pointless for a 13-year-old to fight him on it,
and I came to accept it. After a while I even found myself going
against Pokémon myself, trying to find something to take its place.
But to no avail. I was a simple young man with simple wants and
desires, and my number-one means of entertainment had been
yanked away with no more reason than "Dad said so." I was both-
ered for a long time, and truthfully, still am a little.

While it is easy to say "Honor thy father"; at 13, it was difficult
for me to dive headlong into it. Until then it had been acceptable for
me to play Pokémon. And without warning, it was all gone. Period.
I was still a kid, and I mourned my loss. Over 500 cards, games,

stuffed animals. I knew each Pokémon's strengths and weaknesses, I memorized strategies, I knew who could interact with whom and why or why not. Nothing could replace it fully. But in my heart, I could not dishonor him with a child's game. I pushed my anger down inside.

In time, my dad suggested that my mom wear a veil and cover her arms and legs in public. He also thought it was a good idea that he and I stop wearing hats. He had read that during Biblical times traditionally women wore veils, and men weren't allowed to wear hats in the presence of God. He relaxed on that when my mom said that if she wore a veil then he couldn't go out in public anymore unless every other woman had a veil on as well. She proposed that Dad was trying to make them Muslim. That was enough to change his mind on the matter personally. Although I'm not sure which text he was reading or what he found in the Bible to support it, I didn't wear a hat most of the time because he didn't want me to. He found out later that we did not need to do that. Even though after a while he said he was wrong, he did say he was happy that I respected his wishes. I appreciated that. I would rather have my dad happy than cause his disappointment just because I disagreed with him about something that was more important to him than to me. This was a constant battle inside my head: don't go against Dad, but what if he changes his mind? All those Pokémon, I'd never get them all back.

Pastor Brewster asked Dad to substitute preach at Grace Covenant one week. I was sleeping soundly on Sunday morning when Dad thundered in, his half-buttoned shirt and doo rag still firmly on his head, and no pants, yelling, "Jeremy! Get up! We gotta go! It's already nine o'clock!" Mom and Jecolia weren't home, and we had no one to make certain we were awake and alert. My heart was pounding from the shock of seeing Dad practically bouncing on my bed. He was nudging the mattress with his giant leg. I told him we still had 30 minutes to be on time, but he was frantic. "I have to preach today!" I saw his urgency. I hopped to the closet on one foot, shoving my legs into the first decent pair of pants I found. At that time, dressing perfectly in church wasn't a big issue with my dad (mostly when he wasn't preaching) because he had learned that, traditionally, people weren't dressed up to impress God, but because they thought Constantine, the Roman Emperor responsible for legalizing Christianity, was coming to their church. Since my goal wasn't to impress man, I found a clean pair of jeans and a nice shirt in fewer than two minutes and was downstairs eating a Pop-Tart when my dad came racing downstairs.

On the way to church he said, "I'm sorry I was rushing, but you know how I get when I have to preach. I just want to be on time." The tone in his voice was one I didn't recognize. Not a day in this man's life had I ever known him to be nervous before speaking. Later, when I was 15, I found out he was always nervous. To distract himself, he would swish around the change in his pocket to create noise. And thinking back, I can remember that before almost every single speech he must have been nervous, even if just a little bit.

New Year's Eve 1999. I listened countless times to "Will Y 2K," getting psyched up for the new year. The song was one of the few Dad didn't take issue with. He wasn't big on the whole rap movement. He didn't mind clean rap, but most rap at the time he wasn't down for. He could appreciate artists who had an old-school vibe, like Lauryn Hill, but mostly he listened to '70s music. He liked Will Smith because Will Smith is clean. And early in my house I learned that being clean does not make one soft. My father was clean, and I don't think people wanted to mess with him, am I right?

Early that evening, my parents, my sister, and I invited our extended family and friends to celebrate with us. As we were all conversing, anticipating the 12 o'clock mark, we played the game Guesstures and had a blast debating what was or was not against the rules. Suddenly, the lights went out. All the power in the house had shut off. Everyone's chatter stopped as if it were generated by power too. But after about five seconds I yelled out, "Where's Dad!?!?" It was only 11:35 p.m.; and I realized Dad had been missing about five minutes. As soon as I yelled, the lights and sound burst back on and we could hear Dad laughing from the garage. This man had hit the main power switch, trying to scare us to death. Later, even he said he should have waited until 12 o'clock, but he still had a good laugh. I asked, "Dad, why didn't you just turn off the power switch for the living room?" He said, "I didn't know which one it was, so I just hit the main power." He was laughing about that for the next two weeks. Had I done something like that, Dad probably would have thrown me in the lake. But it was my dad, so who was really going to be mad at him? That night in bed, I realized he had shut down the whole house because my clock was blinking. I laughed thinking, *That's my dad.*

Dad was nominated for Football Player of the Decade at the ESPY Awards. Our family went to Las Vegas. During the awards, Tyra Banks gave an opening speech for the nominees in the category of Best NFL player of the Decade. All my life I had a crush on Tyra Banks, and my mom leaned over to Dad and said, "If you win, maybe you can ask Tyra to take a picture with Jeremy." Since Tyra came out in a bikini top, my dad said, "Not if she has that on." The only disadvantage to my dad's honor was he was the only defensive player nominated. Some of the other nominees were Brett Favre, Barry Sanders, and Jerry Rice. Jerry Rice won the award. After the show, our family made its way to the back where the limousine would pick us up to take us to the hotel. And there she was, Tyra Banks, covered up with a sash so that you couldn't see the bikini top. My mom stopped to ask her if I could take a picture with her. I was a very happy 13-year-old boy.

Turnabout didn't seem like fair play the next day at the airport. Like always, someone recognized Dad. He said kindly, "We're busy. I can't sign autographs. If I sign one for you, I'll have to sign them all. I'm sorry." As a rule, Dad didn't usually sign autographs in public for this reason. As he herded us into the limousine, the eager fan waved his paper and pen at my dad and said, "I thought you were a Christian." My face automatically grimaced like I'd bitten into a sour lemon. *Here it comes.*

I looked out the open car door to see my dad whirl around to the fan and say, "Christian ain't got nothin' to do with it." Sometimes Mom would urge Dad to sign an autograph, especially if it looked as if there wouldn't be a crowd. If a little kid came up to him, he might sign an autograph in public, but after a while, parents caught on and would send their kids over to my dad. I had seen more than one time little kids with paper, leading to the parent, then one more person; and then, if he'd sign three, there'd be 11. He called out that he was sorry and that he couldn't keep going. The fans wouldn't be happy, and they sure wouldn't understand. I would get so mad at them because they didn't care at all that we had things to do.

Beginning in winter of 2000, Dad started to hold Bible studies at Pastor Brewster's church on Wednesday nights. Sometimes I enjoyed going, but other times it seemed like he was repeating himself a lot. The participants learned a lot about sin. For the most part, sin is what he was studying for himself. He found out that little things people considered passable, like exaggeration, was actually a lie, therefore it was a sin. His research found many things to be sinful. He didn't stay on the topic for long; this was not the core of his study. His in-depth studies started to come later once we moved to Charlotte. Dad was really getting into studying the historical part of the Torah. In 2000, we visited Israel for the second time, but this time, we weren't typical tourists. We were experiencing history. We already went through the hustle and bustle of seeing the new sights the first time we went; the second time was more about learning what the sights meant.

We were in Israel and Egypt for ten days. A family friend named R.V. Brown, a big guy with giant triceps, a big voice, and an even bigger heart for God and for people, came on the trip with us. In Israel, when we were inside of a Catholic church, the tour guide asked if anyone in our group wanted to lead the prayer. All in our group looked around knowingly, because if R.V. decided to pray, not only would the church, but the whole country would hear a tremendous roar. The Cathedral would echo loudly if someone were just to speak in a regular voice. R.V. raised his hand and they invited him to come to the altar to pray. R.V. delivered one of the loudest prayers I have ever heard. He was not trying to draw an audience, but when this man gets on fire for God, he inspires everyone listening.

Also in Israel, my cousin Wesley, who was a bit of a troublemaker when he was little, went into a different Catholic church later that week and yelled, "Wow, this is big." Nuns, tourists, and visitors from Israel, praying, being silent, and seeking God privately, turned around to look at him unbelievingly. Had he just stopped there he may not have held an audience, but he went a bit further. Knowing good and well what he was doing because he was an altar boy in his own Catholic church back home, he dipped his fingers into and played in the holy water. A nun swinging a stick chased him, yelling, "This is no picnic!" She ran him out of the church.

When we were leaving Israel, I wanted to take some photographs for my art collage project. I saw a great photo opportunity in the passport computer at the airport because it was written in Hebrew and, for some reason, I was amazed that it wasn't in English. My cousin Wesley told me to make sure I had my flash turned off, but the camera was a cheap one and didn't have that option. I clicked the shot, and things went crazy from there. A security officer approached me and said, "Were you taking a picture of the passport computer?" I tried to explain that I wasn't a spy or anything, but that I was trying to take a picture for my art project. She took me to another set of security guards who confiscated the film in the camera. I started to cry because I was so embarrassed. One security lady did come up to me to say, "It's going to be OK." My dad was right behind me the whole time, ensuring I wasn't going to be taken off to jail.

In Egypt, I thought that it would be fun to see the Pyramids. I was right about that; but that was all I got right about Egypt. An Egyptian asked me if I wanted to take a picture. He offered to put his turban around my head and take a picture with my camera. When I asked him if it was going to cost anything, he said no. I asked him again, and he said no. I agreed, but afterward, of course, he asked for money. I took my camera and kept walking.

There weren't too many things to do in Egypt. We couldn't drink too much of the water because of parasites; but it was hot there, and

**Our visit to the Wailing Wall in Jerusalem
changed our entire family forever.**

I do believe that the flies from the plagues that happened to Egypt so long ago were still there. It was horribly sticky and just downright no fun. None of us liked it. On the way to the airport to leave Egypt, Dad said he felt like Moses leading everyone out of Egypt. Everyone laughed, because they knew it was true. My dad, since he initiated the tour, was Moses, and we, the children of Israel, all wanted to get out of Egypt. "Let my people go," was never before as clear.

When we got back to Ohio, I remembered an Egyptian-themed chess set that I used to play with. A New Jersey friend had given me this expensive handmade set with Looney Tunes characters. There were only 25 like it in the entire world, and each board was autographed. Since I had just seen the Pyramids, I wanted to find that chess set and play with it. I was 14 and not thinking clearly. We had just returned from Egypt, yes, but from where we had learned about what the Pyramids stood for in a traditional sense, what they meant religiously. We learned that most pyramids during early times were made of reflective white limestone to be seen from afar. They were built on the west bank of the Nile River because the sun sets in the west. The pyramid's sun symbolism is shown in its shape, representing the descending sun rays. Most of them are in tribute of the sun god Ra. Also, pyramids' names referenced the sun. All that information was interesting to learn, but I should have realized I shouldn't pull the chess set out of its box immediately after coming home from Egypt. Egypt just reminded me we had it in storage (en route from Green Bay to Charlotte), and I wanted to play some chess with cool characters.

Dad came in and headed for the stairs as I was playing with the set. He glanced in my direction and his footsteps slowed. He seemed to inventory the pieces and then moved on upstairs. Without any discussion or indication, my dad studied these pieces for a few days. He looked at them long and hard before jumping to any rash conclusions. And while he didn't say it, I suspect he prayed on it.

Four days later, our next-door neighbor brought over some of our mail and came by to hear about our trip. Just before he rang the doorbell, Dad had said, "We need to talk about this chess set." After the neighbor left I knew what was coming. During the visit, Dad held Sylvester in his hands as if to prevent him from escape. From an innocent perspective, it was a cute chess set. Sylvester was dressed in a white robe. PePe Lepew and his girl were the Pharaoh and wife on one side, and Bugs Bunny and his girl were the Pharaoh and wife on the opposite side. Yosemite Sam and Marvin the Martian were warriors with dragons on the crests of their shields. Taz and Wile E. Coyote were also in a white robes as wizards. Daffy Duck was a mummy. Pillars were pawns, for one side and pyramids were pawns for the other side. The one monument we saw in Egypt not represented directly on the chess set was the erection of Ra's phallic or sexual organ. If it had, Dad wouldn't have allowed the set to stay as long as it did (To see a genuine replica closer to home, check out the Washington Monument).

Dad exhaled, picking up Daffy Duck for exhibit, and said, "This is a mummy, and you know what the pyramids stand for. And do you know what this is a representation of?" His large hand enveloped a small, defenseless Sylvester the Cat dressed in white linen. Because I didn't want to give in to this conversation, I stalled. I told him I didn't know what it meant.

"It's a magician," he said. "Witchcraft is not taken lightly in this house." And if I waited long enough he'd tell me something else I already knew: Daffy Duck was a mummy, representing rising from the dead. He didn't like the Pharaohs' serpents on their headdresses. Their headdresses undoubtedly anciently symbolized something to do with a false god.

The finality rose over me. I threw them away very hard, literally slamming them into the garbage can. This was the second time in just months that he had taken away something of mine, something that seemed so harmless, and in many ways, was. But countless times Dad said that a house with strife keeps blessings from coming. Pointing a finger he'd say, "And don't keep me from my blessings."

As a peace-keeping measure, Mom replaced the chess set with one of a different theme. Pirates. Before long, Dad was eyeballing the new set, grumbling about the skull and crossbones on every other square. Mom and I quickly covered each offending square with photographs of ourselves.

Another story was nagging his own fear, driving him to literally clean house. He and my mom had heard of a couple who was doing well financially. When they went to Mexico on vacation they bought a statue of a poor Mexican boy. They brought it home and put it up on one of their mantles. Within two weeks, they noticed their stocks start to plummet. Their investments turned sour, and organizations they had supported started to take a turn for the worse. They couldn't figure out what was going wrong. They were God-fearing people, and they prayed. During the prayer, they heard a crash downstairs.

They checked the noise and noticed the statue had fallen off the mantel and broken. Immediately they realized that what they had brought into their house, the representation of poverty, had a "poor" spirit attached to it, causing their decline. From then on, they were very careful about what they brought into their house.

Personally, I agree with that to a degree. I understand why Dad threw out the Egyptian chess set, but I still don't agree with him about Pokémon. My dad had a habit of going overboard when it came to what he felt was right in God's eyes. Instead of going 100 percent, he'd go 150. He was so overly eager to serve God that he wanted to do right by God even if he was more cautious than necessary. But his precaution did not stop here. Sometimes I thought he missed tackling so much that he'd just chosen a different opponent.

It got to the point I was scared to play certain games around him. He even went through my video games and had me throw away certain ones just because of the graphics on the cover. Granted, Twisted Metal 2 did not have the best-looking cover with a wild-haired, smiling clown with blood trickling off his lips, but my dad got straight ridiculous with some things. He looked at Crash Bandicoot and said he didn't like the bad guy from that front cover. I told him it was just the nemesis, and he said, "Well, doesn't that make the game bad?" Dad was out of control; he was clamping down on things that he had no business clamping on. If he saw so much as a hint of an evil face (even if it was not my character) he would say that he didn't like it, and he wanted me to get rid of it. I came to the conclusion that there was no convincing Dad otherwise, so I avoided him at all costs with certain things. It was still the quiet before the storm.

The time came when I actually saw God for myself while living in Ohio, which involved my mom. My dog, G, ran out of the house one afternoon and romped over to our neighbors' yard across the street. He was able to cut corners and was hard to catch. My mom started chasing after him and fell into a small hole in the ground. Even though she felt a pain, she kept going. After she caught G, she came back in the house and said her foot hurt a little. Eight hours later, while Mom and Dad were helping clean out her sister's garage as an anniversary gift, they decided to go to the emergency room and check out her foot. She found out that she had broken it in three places and would need to be off of it for at least four to six weeks to heal. The woman who keeps the house under control and is the backbone of the family was benched for four to six weeks. With Mom on injured reserve, my sister, my dad, and I would all have to step up our game to get things done around the house.

In the next three days, I found out that dad could cook. He can't shop; he bought every spice from the store (which we still have today). And he didn't use any coupons, which made my mom upset; but he could, indeed, cook. We had grilled salmon, and while I didn't like salmon that much, I ate it. With surprise on my face, I kept repeating, "You can cook?!" He looked at me like I was crazy. The truth was out: my dad could cook, he just didn't. He liked to go out to eat, but it was comforting to know that my dad, my father, was able to cook edible food. On that night, that fact stunned me more than all his football records and the impact he made on the game. I talked about it for the next week. Everywhere I went I exclaimed, "My dad can cook! Did you know my dad can cook?!" I think everyone else was as amazed as I was. My dad kept saying, "Yes, Jeremy, I can cook. Now can you stop acting like it is such an amazing thing. I'm not stupid."

I guess sometimes even I could forget he was such a normal guy. However, his cooking would be extremely short-lived, because we were all praying for my mom to get better. None of us expected a miracle, we just wanted her to feel better and heal up. She went to the doctor three days after breaking her foot to get a permanent six-week cast, and she mentioned to the doctor that she felt much better. She told him she thought the Father had healed her. The doctor told her to walk. She reached for her crutches and the doctor said, "You don't need those crutches, do you? The Father healed you, right?" She wasn't sure whether he was being faithful or sarcastic, but Mom jumped off the examination table. No pain. Dad was as excited as a little kid. He stood up and pointed to Mom's foot, crying out, "I knew it! I knew He would heal you!" The doctor then appeased the outrageous couple and took some X-rays. Astonishment covered his face; her X-rays did not look like the same foot in any way from three days before. It was not broken. Broken three days prior, it was not broken now. The doctor said he had never seen anything like it. But it was true. God had healed my mom's broken foot in three days.

This healing is similar to God's healing my father from all those injuries, the most remembered being the torn hamstring that should have ended the season with the Packers, but he came back to play the next week. Mom said she had always prayed for Dad's injuries to be healed, but she never prayed for herself, because she did not feel worthy. But Mom did not need any cast or brace, and she's never had problems with that foot ever since. The doctor couldn't even see fit to charge her for the visit. She says that during that bedridden three days, God told her to slow down and spend more time with Him. She repented and refocused her life.

8

It's been a long road, but we have finally arrived at the last place I will reside with my family until I get out on my own. When I arrived in North Carolina we were not yet living by Lake Norman. Actually, we were still waiting for our house to be built in Cornelius, North Carolina. Fortunately, New York Giants linebacker Michael Barrow and his wife, Shelly, were living in New York during the football season, and they offered us their North Carolina house to live in until our home was finished. During this time we lived in their home in Huntersville, North Carolina. The house was completely furnished with normal-sized furniture, not Reggie White-sized furniture. Dad would have to be careful not to break any more beds.

I wanted to go to public school, which would have been North Mecklenburg. Instead, my mom had other plans, a school that my cousins owned, called Brisbane Academy. There was no need for fussing; it's not like I hadn't been to public school before. I just didn't want to wear uniforms. But, alas, my stint in uniforms wasn't over yet.

Before I actually got to meet anyone, I always wanted to go to Jordan Dean's house. She was the only person I knew in North

Carolina. Our parents relentlessly joked about us getting married some day, but we knew better. But by the end of summer, I began to feel like a burden on her, like she was supposed to entertain me because I didn't know anyone else in North Carolina yet. The best memory of Jordan, though, is when we were visiting them from Green Bay and I was about 12 years old, playing my trumpet; and, for some reason, they asked me to play it outside. I was trying to play "The Star-Spangled Banner" by ear the whole time. I was blaring that horn so loud Jordan's dad said any time the neighbors made him mad, he would just have me bring the trumpet to practice in the backyard. The Dean family still enjoys my musical attempts. I got the talent from my dad who played the tuba in a band when he was younger. In sixth grade, our band held a parents night in which the parents played their kids' instruments. My dad gave everyone quite a show, playing my trumpet to the song "Go Team Go."

I didn't bug Jordan that much, I don't think. The time had come when I worried how the kids at the school were going to accept me. My cousin, who owned the school, let me graduate middle school with them earlier that summer. I had worn a purple suit I had bought in Egypt (for a very good price, I might add). I was the one who was dressed up the most, save one girl who wore business attire. That introduction left me not knowing what they were thinking of me, and they already knew I was Reggie White's son. There was no hiding that. Still, I just wanted to be accepted.

Dad decided to come out of retirement because the Carolina Panthers called and asked him to join the team. They had had some tough seasons, and the news headlines were still hot with Panthers wide receiver Rae Carruth's alleged murder of his pregnant girlfriend the previous year. The trial was oncoming in the middle of that season. The team needed a mature, wise role model to rally the players and to lead in a positive direction. Dad still had some football fight in him and wanted to play.

On the first game at home, the Panthers returned a kickoff for a 92-yard touchdown. My mom was hollering loudly, saying, "Wooo! Yessss! Ninety-two yards. Jeremy, that means something! Ninety-two yards. Yesss!!!" At least she was happy. In another game, the Panthers played the San Diego Chargers when the Chargers weren't so good. But nonetheless, they still were able to block my dad. Dad had rushed the quarterback about four times, and out of those four times he only got one sack. He had one obvious hurry-up, and the rest should have been sacks. If he would have gotten those sacks, if he had not been half a step off, he would have had three sacks that game instead of one. On the ride home he said, "Man, I should have had those sacks." The only reason he got the one was the quarterback tripped (not to take anything away from my dad; it's just a fact). He was still a dominant player, but he wasn't the rookie he used to be. Dad realized he had slowed down. I think that might have frustrated him the most.

My dad was a huge advocate for not bringing a negative turnout of a football game home with him. He didn't want it to affect his attitude toward the family or his friends (other than his teammates). There was one game, though, he commented on quite a bit because of a call by the referee in the Panthers stadium.

The Panthers had caused a fumble and went to grab the football. A defensive player grabbed it but got pushed in the process while still on his feet. He fell into and then out of the back of the end zone. The referees called a safety, giving the Falcons two points against the Panthers. My dad was outraged by this. After the game, my dad kept stressing, "That should have never been called as a safety because the player's momentum took him into the end zone." When I talked to my Aunt Maria about this later that week, she boldly stated, "A rule is a rule, and momentum or not, he was in the end zone and then went out of the end zone; therefore, it is a safety."

Aunt Maria and her family had just moved to North Carolina about 15 minutes away from where we were staying while our house was built. Our families were close to each other. About a year later, my maternal grandparents would come to live right by my family and my aunt's family.

On the first day of school, I forgot what I was so worried about. This was the first time in my life, however, that I was in the same classroom as my sister. Since the school was small (73 people in K-12), seventh through ninth grades were held in the same classroom. My ninth grade year still felt like middle school, even though I was technically in high school.

At first it didn't seem so bad. Every student had an Apple iBook with a wireless card to access the Internet during class assignments and to facilitate research and writing. It was fun, especially Instant Messenger, when we started telling each other how boring classes were while the teacher was teaching. The word on Napster spread quickly when people started saying the word "free" around school. I wasn't all that into music at the time. Sure, there were things I liked and what-not, but I wasn't into what was popular, especially in hip-hop, rap, or R&B. I was a real stickler, and I didn't want any of my music to have cursing in it. And I didn't want to hear it if it did. But when I got on Napster I started finding clean versions of some songs that I did like, and I started finding a lot of songs I had grown up liking, but had never bought the CD. It was great; I typed in the name of a song and, just like that, it was up for me to download.

When Napster started making the front pages each day about going to court over copyright infringement, my teacher told us how free music was going to be taken away. We started downloading like crazy. We made it a competition and asked each other, "How many songs do you have?" One of us might have 74 songs, the next girl had 121 songs, and the next guy had 180. Once the administration found out we were downloading music at school, they made us sign a contract stating that we "understood" that we are not supposed to download music, and that is not what the computers at school were to be used for. After I signed the contract and continued to download music, a friend of mine said, "Jeremy, you're lying. You just signed that contract." I said, "But the contract said that I 'understand'; it didn't say I wouldn't do it." Then everybody started jumping on board with my interpretation. Fortunately, we never got in trouble. I became wiser in high school and decided not to participate anymore, especially when my mom found out.

I was obsessed with one music artist, Stacie Orrico. She only had released a debut album, but I read every website she had consented; I had a crush. My dad knew I was totally obsessed with her and, on one of his business trips, he ran across a man who knew Stacie's father. When he came home to find me in my room doing my homework he said, "Hey, look what I was able to get." I looked at him in disbelief as he held Stacie Orrico's autograph. I was at a loss for words. This was one of the few times I loved the fact that my dad was famous and had connections. I was elated.

One friend from school liked hanging out at our house. I wasn't the nicest person to Marvin. I enjoyed being around him, and we did a lot of stuff outside school together; but I was annoyed when my mom would invite him over without telling me. It wasn't that I didn't want him there, but I felt like Mom was dropping him on me to entertain. That's how I thought I might have been imposing on Jordan Dean when we first moved to North Carolina. I copped attitudes and protested when she set these play dates for me. One day in mid-resistance, my mom said, "Jecolia said she would hang out with him." And Marvin grinned, "Yeah, Jermy (he said it like my name was Germy) I'm just gonna hang out with your sister, since she is my future wife and all." He said it in the silliest tone, not sarcastic at all. My mom just knew he loved coming over and she kept inviting him. After a while he was part of the family.

Marvin and I did have a good time together in my ninth-grade year. He and I were on the same very good recreational basketball team. Early in the season we played a decent team. It literally came down to the final seconds of play when Marvin hit the last shot with about 17 seconds left. We held their offense long enough and won the game. On the court, I grabbed Marvin and held him up while he shook his fist, saying, "Yeah, yeah, yeah." No one else seemed to be as enthused, maybe because it was only a community league. Nonetheless, I had pride in my win and in my friend who made the game-winning shot.

Dad came to one game, but he brought a book and was barely watching the game. This book was about the Bible, no doubt. He was so enthralled with learning new things about the Bible and God and the Hebrew language that he would even try to get a little learning time in during my games. I remember wondering why he even came if he was just going to read a book. Didn't he care enough to watch me? He was already at football practice all day, just like the entire time I was growing up. Couldn't he act just a little interested in what was going on in my life?

If I had been older, I would have understood what he was reading and beginning to understand in his own life; and I wouldn't have been so apt to judge. But that is hindsight. And all the money in the world can't afford that. I was in ninth grade, headlong in my self-absorbed, young teenage life. I had supported Dad and all his practices and games, all his trips for appearances and preaching, all the moves from house to house, upsetting my own plans and my own schedules for 14 years.

As my back pain receded, I started to play basketball more. Since in the community league everyone made the playoffs, we went on to sweep the playoff series and go to the championship game. But in that final game, we played like a team that didn't deserve to be there. We were getting beat all over. We weren't running back on defense, and we let Marvin go down the court by himself on a break-away. I couldn't box out to save my life, and a player on their team was rebounding, hitting shots, and almost dunking on us a few times. They whipped us. I was so sad about second place I almost started to cry. Whatever the age, the big game, whether it's community league, high school, college, or the pros, is played to win. And if not, why play? Even Dad admitted to crying when the Packers lost to Dallas, knocking out their shot at the playoffs in 1995.

We went out to eat with some family friends. We went to Buffalo's for wings. I was excited because they had at least 15 different flavors of buffalo sauce to choose from or mix and match. It usually took 15 minutes at most to get our food when we went. Taking into account that we had five more people in our group that day, I factored in another five minutes for food. We should have had our food in about 20 minutes. The problem was it took an hour for our food to come out. Any reasonable person would question this delay. The restaurant was not crowded, and we didn't order food that was difficult to make. Our waiter kept apologizing to us. Every time we asked him about the food, he would say, "I'm sorry. I'm so sorry." His demeanor showed real remorse. After the food came, we ate happily, still curious why it took so long to get our order. We would get our answer shortly.

When we walked outside, immediately I saw it. Two men were standing outside the door, with about four regular-sized Green Bay helmets, a couple of mini-helmets, and two footballs. They came up to my dad, markers ready, and asked him to sign the items that they hoped would soon be memorabilia. My dad turned them down, saying, "I'm with my family right now. I don't do this when I'm with my family."

As we got into the car, my mom didn't ask why he didn't sign it for them; she already knew. Mostly, when my mom coaxed my dad into signing something it was usually for a child. This time she knew full well what had happened. I said, "Wow, they sure were carrying around a lot of stuff to be 9:30 at night." Dad said, "You think they were just walking around with that stuff, Jeremy? Naw, I know what happened. One of them had a buddy at the restaurant and he probably told them, 'I'll call you the next time Reggie is here so you can come get him to sign some of your stuff for your store.' The reason they kept us there for an hour was because the two guys probably couldn't get there until later; and the restaurant manager kept our food purposely until they could arrive and ask me to sign their stuff. Well, I wasn't gonna sign anything."

I thought that was so messed up. But it made sense and was most likely true. Why else were two guys right outside of the restaurant we were eating in near 9:30 at night and carrying a lot of Green Bay Packer memorabilia with them?

Dad was starting to learn more about his walk with God. First he learned to implement the observance of the Sabbath. He would quiz me with questions like, "Jeremy, what's the seventh day of the week?" I would tell him it was Saturday. Then he would ask, "So why do we observe the Sabbath on the first day of the week?" This is typical dad operation in his teachings. He would ask questions to steer the person's thinking on the subject rather than straight-out tell them what he believes. Another question he often asked was, "How many commandments are there?" When I told him ten he would ask, "Well, why is it that we only observe nine? One of the commandments is to 'Remember the Sabbath day and keep it holy.'" This lesson always came when he thought we were doing something inappropriate.

On those Saturdays we slept in, we had Bible study, and when it was over at 6 p.m. (because Biblical days ran from sundown to sundown), we would go to the movies and out to eat as a family. Little else qualified as acceptable. My dad wanted to serve God so much he went to extremes, very respectable and, at the same time, annoying. When my dad started "enforcing" the Sabbath on us, as I choose to call it now, I did not like it very much.

We couldn't watch television, I couldn't play video games, we couldn't even pour cereal into a bowl. We very nearly couldn't heat up any food in the microwave, but I reasoned with Dad that putting food into the microwave wasn't like cooking in the old days. Back then, one had to chop the wood, make a fire, hunt for the food, catch it, etc. It was work. Still, we couldn't buy anything, not even a soda from the soda machine. We couldn't play in our basketball games on Saturdays. It got so bad I was asking to listen to music on the Sabbath. Before this decree, Saturday used to be my favorite day. Now, I was in school five days, in prison for one, and finally I had a day off, Sunday. But I couldn't even fully enjoy Sunday, because I knew school was the next day. The Sabbath had turned into a day I dreaded instead of a day I loved. My resentment started to build. It started with Pokémon, but because I am a person who doesn't like confrontation, I never went against my dad. But each day the resentment grew.

Another thing Dad stopped when I was 15 was Christmas. Most were probably thinking our family was confused between being Jehovah's Witness and Jewish, but we were neither. Simply my dad looked into the origins of Christmas and Easter, and he didn't like what he saw. I felt my world crashing down—the end of Christmas, prison day-camps on Saturday, and a father I couldn't confide in because I was always afraid of his response. Certainly, I wasn't afraid he would become violent, but he seemed so unreasonable. That Christmas we gradually did away with the traditions. We did open gifts, but we didn't have a Christmas tree. When Dad retired from Green Bay, football practice turned into spiritual practice, and he gave it everything he had. He was constantly reading books on Hebrew and scriptural commentary; and this illumination caused Dad to turn scrutiny onto himself.

The more Dad learned, the more Dad talked. But instead of growing proud and exultant, he grew upset, because people he knew and trusted, the very people who helped him in his own spiritual walk years ago, told him they knew about the origins of Christmas and Easter but ignored them. This disregard hurt my dad so much. He felt lied to. Even though he wanted to do right by God, I'm sure he was doing certain things because he didn't want to be like the people he was so mad at.

He found that a Christmas tree could be viewed as an idol. The 25th was not Jesus' birthday because, according to the Hebrew calendar he was born sometime in October. Different "signs" of Christmas: the holly, the wreath, the mistletoe, none had implications to do with Jesus or Christianity. My dad didn't want us to have anything to do with it. It was a sad December day when my sister and I were trying to be happy, knowing my dad was hating every minute of it. Like normal, we minimized it and didn't show our disappointment.

I did get a Play Station 2 out of the whole thing. I remember I found it before I was to open it. To see PS2 in that cool font on the front of that big blue box was something great. Of course I told my mom I saw it, but we still saved it for the last Christmas we ever had.

When we asked other Christians, they admitted that December 25 wasn't the day either; however, they didn't do any research about the solstice and how Constantine legalized Christianity, coinciding the new holiday with the pagans' winter solstice to facilitate the transition to Christianity.

By the second year we skipped Christmas, the whole family felt relief by December 26. We had avoided the stressful preparation, and we didn't have the massive clean-up that everyone around us had, not the piles of wrapping paper and boxes, not the refrigerator stuffed with leftover food, not the dying tree and all its decorations. We knew that the Messiah was not born on that day, and we thought about that in relation to the question, "What if we had just picked a random day to celebrate any one of our birthdays?" I know I would be offended if Mom had just picked a day in August to celebrate my May birthday. Isn't that the same thing? It was not up to us to celebrate Yeshua's (the Hebrew name of Jesus) birthday on December 25, when we know in the scriptures it speaks about during the Feast of Tabernacles that it was fall when He was born.

After the third year with no White Christmas, we had absolutely no celebration, and we were looking at other folks with sympathy. The rest of the world was going through all of the materialism of the season, but they continued to be taught a lie spiritually. About every other day, during December, Dad grumbled about how most pastors know it is a lie but they can't change the church tradition. It really disappointed my parents that some of our closest pastor friends told us that they would lose their congregation if they preached the truth about the things we were studying. Preaching to the membership list was hypocrisy, and Dad would have none of that.

When I played football at school, I tried to emulate my dad's honor on the field. We all played, even the girls sometimes. Even though some of them didn't quite know what a touchdown was, they were still into it. One time in particular there was a girl playing on my team named Bianca. We were down by a touchdown and we needed to tie up the game. There wasn't a very good chance that we were going to do it, because the teams seemed kind of lopsided. If I recall correctly it was third down, so even if we had missed we would have had another chance to score.

Before the play I told Bianca to go back to the end zone because no one was going to be expecting me to pass to her. She said she didn't want me to throw to her, I told her to just do it. When the ball was hiked to me, everyone ran toward the end zone. Some other players on my team did curls where they just went out and came back, not fully going for the touchdown. I looked, and there she was, Bianca, all alone in the end zone. The biggest question, however, was whether or not she would be able to catch it. I didn't spend too much time thinking about this, I just lobbed it up there to her. It was a perfectly thrown pass that came down right where she was. No one expected her to catch it, so no one on the other team tried to go for the interception.

I was almost positive she was going to drop it too, and then I heard a THUMP. It was so loud. I kept looking at her, and she had caught the ball like she was holding a baby. I immediately shouted for joy as if it were the comeback of the century. Everyone's faces reflected the same question: How in the world did this girl catch the ball? Well she caught it, and that's all that mattered. People could say it was luck, people could say it was dumb luck, people could even say it was just crazy stupid dumb luck, but you know, luck or not, it happened, and that was a big highlight for me in my ninth-grade, lunch-break football career.

During lunch time I would also go visit my friends in Pre-K. I used to see the little four-year-olds in their classroom. I've always loved kids and been able to get along with them. One boy named Amari was cute but mischievous. It was funny listening to the kids call the teacher, Lynn Clark, "T-shirt" for "teacher." I was similar to my dad in that he always became the clown around a group of kids. I enjoy being that for a lot of kids. I was the one they could play around with, and I didn't mind that one bit.

After football season, we got on the basketball court. Since the school was small, we only had a one-goal basketball court, and we played 21. For some reason I was better than I thought I would be. Because I was so tall, I could just grab all the rebounds from my fellow classmates. I hit most of my shots because of the backboard. I didn't care about looking good; points are points. People used to always try to get under my skin saying, "You killin' that backboard, ain't you?" I would respond with, "But I'm winnin', though, ain't I?" My competitive nature came from my father. One day, Dad, a few guy friends, and I were at the rec center, playing a game of 21. When my dad shot the ball, it bounced off the rim and went out of bounds toward my mom. She tried to grab it and throw it to me. My dad was enraged. He said, "Sara, stop messing up the game! You can't just give him the ball like that!" Son or no son, for those minutes we were playing 21, I was his opponent.

In one game, the rebound came off and went toward the playground. One of my classmates, Ricardi, got to the loose ball at the same time I did, and we started tussling. I didn't expect him to put up much of a fight. He was by no means a small or weak guy. We scuffled for a good 30 seconds before I finally won. Later, some of us adventurous types went outside to play tackle football. In the seventh grade, my sister was my height. She would play with us. With Ricardi on one team and Jecolia on the other, we just gave the ball to both of them, and no one could, or wanted to tackle, either of them. Especially in the cold when it hurt to hit or be hit, we just let them run. Within ten minutes the score of that game was close to 40 each.

We also had our times to get on each other's nerves. One time in gym we played kick ball. Unfortunately, we played in the grass. The grass wasn't short and was slowing up the ball during the pitch. My sister, the aggressive athlete, got into some argument with a guy named Jonathan. Things were said, comments were made, regular faces turned into contorted, arguing faces; and by the end of it, Jonathan had flipped off Jecolia. Needless to say, this was the first such gesture Jecolia ever received. It made her so mad that she told my dad about it at home, but somehow he understood that it was partly her fault because she had been in an argument with him.

That's the first time anything like that ever happened to my sister. It bugged her for a little while, and usually things don't bother her like that. She's more like my dad and is able to brush things off. Before this incident, I had never seen anything get to her that much. Thankfully, later Jonathan apologized to her, and everything was good between them.

At the end of the year the school gave out different awards to students who excelled in their subjects or in individual classes. I got awards in Spanish, math, and history. While it was a good year at Brisbane, I knew I was not going back there the next year. It wasn't the school for me. I didn't quite know where I was going, but I didn't want to be in another private school.

Throughout ninth grade, I babysat my grandfather's bird, a small green parrot with a red face. This bird, Cherry, was a gift that we actually gave my grandmother, but it became my grandfather's bird. He loved it. Cherry loved my grandfather, my uncle Steve, and me for as far back as I can remember. Everyone else he didn't like so much.

Another bird occupied my ninth grade year. In Tampa that January, we went to Universal Studios and Disney World. Because my father gave a 20-minute interview with ESPN Club, we had a tour guide. A close family friend, Mrs. Bonita Pulido took me to a pet store where I saw an African Grey Parrot. I liked the bird so much and learned that they are the smartest parrots in the world. One can have a 300-word vocabulary on its own accord. I wanted one. My mom asked me if I was willing to give up G, my Pomeranian, for the African Grey, and I told her yes. The Pomeranian was stubborn, and his favorite place to "go" was the white carpet. Little did I know that my dad would surprise me with the bird, and he bought my sister a parakeet too. At first, I named this bird Alexia because I thought it was a girl, but when I found out it was a boy I just left his name Lexi. We still have him today, and he is smart and faithful.

In July, my dad wanted to surprise my mom with a little ceremony that she would never forget. My dad told me in June and said,

"I'm going to put a wedding renewal together for Mom and me, but this time, it's going to be similar to how they did weddings in the Bible. But you can't tell her, OK?"

I said ok and did what every self-involved 15-year-old does: I forgot all about it. My dad did such a good job planning it, that one week before the event, he mentioned he was still doing it, which surprised me. I'm not saying he was incompetent, but I thought something as big as a wedding, even a renewal, would be a lot for my dad to handle. I later found out that Aunt Maria, my mom's older sister, helped out a lot with it.

I remember that day like it was yesterday. I was wearing the purple suit I had bought in Egypt. I know, that's pretty slick. I looked like I had been in on it the entire time. A lot of people were invited to the renewal, and there were some friends from Green Bay and New Jersey that I hadn't seen in years. We held the renewal on our driveway by our house. Close to 100 people were able to attend. Just before it began, my dad realized my mom was coming. He was wound up. He hushed everyone. "OK, everybody, Sara's coming."

When Mom walked into the ceremony she was all smiles. She was truly stunning. I had never seen my mom look so beautiful. I remember thinking I was glad she is my mom and Dad had pretty good taste. One of our good friends tricked her into trying on a wedding dress earlier that day, and that was her clue that something was going on. Little did she know that she would be having a Biblical (more commonly understood as a Jewish) wedding. My mom and dad had a Katuba, a marriage contract between two people in the Bible made for them. They had a prayer shawl stretched over their heads, and they broke the wine glass at the end of the ceremony.

It looked eerily similar to a Jewish wedding; but my dad reassured the audience that it was simply a Biblical wedding. Hey, it's not his fault that one group keeping up with the traditions of the Bible is Jewish. But to Dad, the ceremony was the way people held weddings in the Bible, nothing more, nothing less. My dad was not trying to run away from calling what he did Jewish, because he did-n't believe they were. He didn't think it was an accurate stereotype to say if he was doing the Feasts of the Lord in the Old Testament and keeping the commandments of the Old Testament and the tra-ditions of the men living during that time that he must be Jewish. God gave all those things to "His children." All of us believers are "His children." He didn't like people to think the Old Testament was Jewish.

My dad really loved that he could give my mom that renewal. It really touched him. He kept saying, "We haven't gotten into an argu-ment since the renewal. I figure, hey, if we ever get into another argument, we're having another renewal." The reason he liked it so much wasn't simply because it was a Biblical wedding, but that he was able to surprise the woman he loved. I get my romantic side from my father, no question about that. Seeing all the sweet things he would do for Mom, I always looked at them and said, "I'm even going to do that for the woman I love and marry. One day I'm going to do it better."

And what I've found out is that women like that. All those guys that think they always have to be "hard" and not show any emotion, are leaving more women to choose from for us. Romance is a real A+ in many girls' minds, even if they don't show it at first. Look at my dad. He should be testament enough after getting the beautiful woman that he sought and pursued for a year.

One day Uncle Walter came to pick me up to hang out with my cousins. We had just moved to North Carolina, and he said they would show me around. We had plans to go to the mall, play some basketball at the rec center, and have a barbecue at his house. My dad's half-brother's family lived in nearby Charlotte, and I didn't know them that well. On the way to their house, Walter, who obviously didn't know me very well either said arrogantly, "Now, I don't want you going around saying, 'I'm Reggie White's son!'"

Without hesitation, I told him flat out, "I don't go around doing that. You don't gotta worry about that." That offended me. I know the kind of person I am and how I was raised to act; and clearly he didn't know me or my family too well if he expected me to act like a brat. Today, I've lived near Charlotte for almost five years. We don't see Walter any more regularly than we did then, and there are still many people who don't know I am Reggie White's son.

From the time I was 13 until 16, Dad was a regular game-show host, always asking questions, "Did you ever think about Jesus' halo?" and "Do you know where the image of Jesus came from?" *I know the halo represented the pagan Sun god, not the radiance of God. I know the image of Jesus we have is either the painter's brother or some random guy sitting in; but stop with the questions. Just tell us what you want us to know.* I thought it, but I couldn't say it.

"Did you ever wonder why this passage in Matthew says one thing and in Mark it says another?"

"No, Dad."

"They changed the wording. Matthew was originally written in Hebrew. Didn't you think it was strange when it read that you don't need to keep the laws of Moses? The English translation left out a word that changed it." These trivia games took place mostly in the car, because he knew we couldn't get away. Otherwise, he might get his feelings hurt.

During the summer of 2001, my father met a rabbi named Ralph Messer. We went to Colorado to visit him and his family. His son, who was about 19 years old, had these tassels hanging from his pants. When I asked him if those were tzit tzits, he told me they were. I asked him if I could have one. The man gave me all four. In the Bible, God told the children of Israel to wear strings, tzit tzits, on their clothing to remind them to keep the commandments. Tzit tzits are the little strings hanging off the four corners of a prayer shawl. I wore them all throughout tenth grade.

While in Colorado, I heard one of Rabbi Messer's sermons. He talked a lot about Torah, why the commandments are important to keep, and the roots of certain Hebrew words in the Bible that most people wouldn't regularly know. I enjoyed it very much; his sermon moved me. So much, in fact, I outright told my dad, "Dad, I wanted to rebel so bad before when you were teaching me all this stuff, but after listening to Rabbi Ralph, that was one of the best things I have ever heard." Surprisingly, my dad did not get mad or upset, but excited. He got so excited that he bragged to people about what I said. That I wanted to rebel, but I didn't. He was extremely proud of that. Go figure.

9

When I got to Southshore I didn't know anyone, nor anyone who had ever been to that school. In my first class, biology, we were excused for an assembly to have Krispy Kreme doughnuts and to meet people in our grades. Everyone was mingling, getting to know one another and asking each other about summer vacation, when two girls came up to me. They asked me that same question I didn't want to be asked or ever answer in my life. No greetings. No introductions. Just "Is Reggie White your dad?" I said yes. I said yes like I was caught in an interrogation. This is the only question in the world I would not mind lying about. But they would find out eventually. They started saying how cool it was and how tall I was compared to them and blah, blah, blah. Whatever else they said didn't matter; they thought they *knew* somebody now.

Before moving on, it should be noted that I was the only black kid in high school. Not that this makes a big difference, but after being around black people at Brisbane, I did feel singled out at this school. But that wouldn't be the defining reason I was singled out.

Everything seemed normal so far. As I got into my classes, I knew Bible class would prove to be interesting. Fortunately, I was placed in ninth-grade Bible because my other classes conflicted with the tenth-grade class. I'm still thankful for the scheduling conflict, because it would have been everyone versus Jeremy White. This Bible class full of ninth graders who didn't like to think. I wasn't threatened by them.

Southshore was cool for about two weeks. The first foul thing that happened was an invitation to the movies for about seven of us to go see *Rush Hour 2*. When my mom dropped me off at the movies only one girl showed up, no one else. The movie was a bit awkward, because I didn't know her at all. The girl and I sat a seat apart. Come Monday I asked two of the girls who were supposed to go why they didn't show up. With a half-bubbly, half-snotty attitude they said, "We should have told you if we didn't go no one was going to show up. We're the popular ones." What?! There were only 17 people in my entire tenth grade class. How do you separate popular from unpopular with 17 people? Shouldn't everyone be friends, even in the slightest form? That's how it was at Green Bay Christian. With 30 people in my class we all at least got along. There weren't any straight-up outcasts. Coming into Southshore, this was new and unexpected, especially for a small Christian school.

Within the first month, the high school students went on a retreat for further bonding and development. I thought this retreat would help me really get to know others like me. Later, I would come to find out these people were nothing like me. Within the first night, most kids found out that I didn't eat pork. They knew this because three guys and I got together to talk about the Bible, as we were instructed.

After we sat down, I asked them why we don't keep some of the commandments in the Old Testament. A guy named Tim asked me to give him a specific commandment. I pointed out that it says, "Do not tattoo your bodies," in Leviticus. He told me that it had to do with mourning for the dead. But I refuted it does not state "in mourning for the dead," it just states "Do not tattoo your bodies." I pointed out that it says, "You shall not make any cuttings in your flesh, for the dead, neither shall you make in yourselves any figures or marks: I am the Lord." in Leviticus 19:28. I explained it states in another part of the sentence, "Neither shall you make in yourselves any figures or marks."

Another point I made was concerning to the food laws and keeping kosher. Tim showed me Acts 10. At that time, I did not know the whys of the commandments, only the don'ts. I knew not to do something even when I didn't know why I shouldn't, because I trusted my father. My father told me, concerning Acts 10, that the dream Peter had in which God told him not to call things unclean that he has made clean didn't allow people to eat whatever they wanted. From that explanation, I told Tim that I wasn't sure how, but Acts 10 was not about food, it was about a person.

That day would haunt me until I figured out exactly what to tell Tim in how food laws still apply to us today. "Jeremy doesn't eat meat," was all they could take from the new kid that night. A few days after we returned, the staff assigned every student to a club. Instead of a service or buddy club, they put me in Bible club. I don't know whether they were interested in what I would say in meetings, or whether they thought they could change some of my beliefs; but after the retreat, I just thought it was ironic.

After the retreat, I invited to my house some kids to get acquainted with whom I hoped to call my future friends. Of the seven people I called, three showed up. I should have thought about what I was doing before I did it. First, some people felt left out, and some thought I was being rude for not inviting them. Second, my house was huge, and their first impression of me was my house and my dad. After escorting them in, one girl said, "Whoa, I just need a minute to take all this in." Suddenly I felt like I was entertaining a bunch of strangers whose sole purpose in being there was to say they had been to my house.

We watched only part of a movie in the theater room before they had to leave. By Monday morning, everyone had heard that I invited them over my house. At least four people said to me, "I hear you have heated seats in the bathroom." Trying to be modest I said, "Yeah, but my mom got them basically for free." None of the three who came over was I ever close with. Normally, I keep those kinds of people away from me with a kind of Reggie White radar. But I was trying to fit in.

On Labor Day weekend, Heather Wehner, my Jersey babysitter, had grown up and was getting married the same time my dad was being honored in Philadelphia as a former Eagle. I didn't want to go, because I was tired of traveling. I just wanted to be able to have a nice three-day weekend at home. And I wanted to possibly be at home to hang out with a girl I had a little bit of interest in. When I was told I had to go, I wasn't thrilled.

This was the first wedding my dad officiated that he used the name *Elohim* to refer to God, rather than using just *God*. He did this in front of a lot of people who had no idea what he was talking about or why. It was kind of embarrassing to me, because I thought he wanted to be different just for the sake of being different. Later, I came to understand that my dad wanted to serve God so badly that he didn't care if his whole life and language were changing, as long as he honored God in a respectable and genuinely humble way.

By my tenth grade year, Dad started to let up some on our Sabbath restrictions, as I liked to think of them. He still had a bit of a problem with our participation in sports on Saturdays, but he didn't demand we stay home. That was an intensive year for my dad to start to learn Hebrew. Because he already had an interest sparked in the commencement of certain traditions, now he embarked on learning the Hebrew language.

Every time I went into that class, I dreaded it. I always took a defensive approach, even before I got into the classroom. Once second semester came, I knew I would be out of there and in a different club, one where I did not have to worry about being attacked for my beliefs. Even though I was able to give Biblical evidence for a belief, I still had to fight off these programmed Christians.

One time I mentioned we light candles on the Sabbath, and one kid asked me if we were taking part in a seance. They were very uncomfortable thinking for themselves; and anything that went against what they had already been taught was impossible for them to consider. Another time I tried to explain to a boy that the snake

Dad always had me on his lap, especially when I was being a little wild at times.

Jecolia and I dressed alike all the time. I think my mom thought we were twins. Dad loved to make us laugh and make funny faces for his photos.

We often used Dad's chest as a pillow. We both loved to snuggle on his chest because he made us feel so secure.

Mom always said I was a cute little boy. I agree!

We are at the Pro Bowl hanging out. He worked most of the day, but we always had dinner together.

My dad was the biggest kid. Here is his demonstration of a life preserver. He always had to go to our Copeland family reunion every year at Myrtle Beach. Funny thing is, he didn't even like the beach. I guess it was our family.

Dad was always giving us horseback rides. Here we are with Willie and Danniesse Gault's daughter, Shakari. Willie Gault and my father were very close friends.

Jecolia, Dad, and I were outside of our New Jersey neighborhood taking snapshots. Of course, Mom has the camera again.

Here we surprised Dad on his 25th birthday at his radio show with Neil Hartman in Philadelphia. We brought Coach Buddy Ryan with us, too.

Mom loved to take photos. I think she may have thought I was interested in football because of my helmet. Jecolia looks a bit uncomfortable.

Brett and Dad always had jokes while riding the bus. Red shared this photo with me. Dad, Red, and Brett were always clowning.

Mom was baptized in the Jordan River by Dad and Pastor Michael Dudley.

I held my nose while Dad dunked me in the Jordan River. Pastor Dudley and Dad had the honor of baptizing everyone.

While in Israel, we were
encouraged to keep journals.
I never saw my dad write
so much.

I enjoyed keeping a journal, too. I noted all of my experiences in Jerusalem.
Israel was like home, and we enjoyed it tremendously.

Jecolia, me, my mom, and Amy are enjoying the Eagles celebration
for my dad's number retirement.

We were in a parade after we won the Super Bowl. Chattanooga also named a street after my dad.

We are taking a family photo at our new home in Lake Norman.
Photo courtesy www.ladianne.com—Ladianne Mandel

I taught at Gateway Academy my last two years in high school, I came back to see some of my kids all grown up. I often visit them during my college breaks.

Brett Favre, me, and my mom at a book signing following the induction ceremony.

Mom posed with John Madden and Rayfield Wright at the Hall of Fame.
We all became like family.

We got to spend a lot of time with the players during the induction weekend, especially Warren Moon.

Mom and Grandpa pose for a photo by the field after the Hall of Fame game.

Cousins Wes, Jamal, and Grandpa met Bill Willis, who was the first black player to play in the NFL. It was the highlight of my grandpa's week.

Mom and I celebrate after the enshrinement in the media room in Green Bay.

My mother and I pose under a giant poster of my father at the Green Bay induction ceremony.

At the Green Bay induction ceremony with George Koonce (middle) and Reggie McKenzie (right).

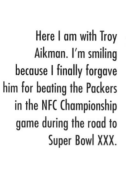

Here I am with Troy Aikman. I'm smiling because I finally forgave him for beating the Packers in the NFC Championship game during the road to Super Bowl XXX.

John Madden poses for a photo with me. Dad loved Mr. Madden, and I found out that Mr. Madden loved my dad just as much.

My cousin, Wes, and I show off our sharp clothes before dinner.

Wesley and Jecolia actually dressed up for the enshrinement. They looked beautiful.

Mom, Granddaddy, cousin Jamal, and I pose with a few Eagles players at our brunch before the game. We had a lot of fun reminiscing about Dad.

My mom, me, and Jecolia pose for a family moment.

Mom handed me the beautiful framed plaque in honor of my dad. I enjoyed raising it up
to celebrate his life and his legacy.

The 2006 Pro Football Hall of Fame inductees pose for a shot on stage.

in Genesis was not Satan. I proved it to him through scripture, but he just told me, "Well, I don't agree with you. You're wrong."

Other times the conversation itself revolved around my tzit tzits and my not eating certain foods. I remember feeling so mad at myself when I told my fellow classmates that *Gentile* did not mean that someone wasn't Jewish but someone who was pagan. They looked it up in *Webster's* and told me it said, "Someone who is not a Jew." When I got home I was so angry that I looked it up myself, and the second definition was indeed, "pagan." I realized then that we were both partially right. In those days, gentiles did not believe in the God of Abraham, Isaac, and Jacob; therefore, they were indeed pagans. I wanted to go back and show them the truth. Alas, I could not and would have to move on. *Wait 'til they hear we don't celebrate Christmas!*

Then the day came that all Americans will remember forever. I was sitting in my geometry class when the principal came over the loudspeaker to announce that there had been a terrorist attack on the World Trade Center in New York, September 11, 2001. The first thing that I thought was, *Who cares? There are a lot of bad things that happen around the world. Why is this cause for someone to get on the intercom and announce a terrorist attack? Don't bad things in this country happen to innocent people every day? What makes this so special?*

Of course as soon as I went into my English class and saw the commotion on television I knew why. The mood at school mirrored the mood of the country that day, chaotic and grim. Students were crying and calling home to leave early. I was just glad no one I knew was there. But wait... My dad was in New York. Deep down I felt he was probably all right, but I had to know for sure. Before I could call out of the school, Mom called to tell me she had heard from him, and he was fine. On a day as cataclysmic as this that would bring the whole nation together if even for a while, my English teacher still gave us homework.

Going home, all I could think about was turning on the news to watch and hoping that Mom would grab a newspaper because this would be something to show my children one day. I knew I was living through something of historical significance. When I got home, Mom said Dad wanted to get home so badly, but all the flights were grounded. He even tried to rent a car or take a bus. My mom told me they had shut down some of the bridges in New York. We didn't know when he was going to get back. Knowing he was safe was enough. It felt like he was just at an away game.

Growing up, I really never missed my dad a whole lot like people would imagine. I wasn't used to him always being there, and it was easier not to miss him. One time in Green Bay, he asked me if I missed him while he was away, and I said yes (he was expecting the usual "No"). I actually did miss the guy. But on September 11, 2001, since I knew he was safe, I didn't worry about it too much. The next day my mom said the people he was visiting offered to drive him to Charlotte. He was so eager to get back and be with us, he took them up on that offer. Had he not been late that morning, he was sched-uled to attend a meeting at the Marriott, blocks away from the Twin Towers, things could have turned out differently.

Finally fall break came. Even though school started on August 6, we had a week off in October. My family went to Florida to Universal Studios and Disney World. My dad's boycott of Disney because of their support of homosexuality had finally ended. While in Florida, I had a great time, and I would also start something that would live on for a while. I would decide that I wanted to grow my hair out so that I could get it braided. I didn't run this by anyone really, especially my dad. I didn't want him to tell me I couldn't. He had already vetoed my long hair in sixth grade. I figured I wouldn't say anything, and maybe he wouldn't notice.

After fall break, our family took a trip to Oklahoma to what became one of the best spiritual times in my life. I found out I was not alone in the way I believed in the Bible. We went to the Feast of Tabernacles, or Sukkot, a holiday commanded by God in the Old Testament for the children of Israel, or God's people, to keep. It was exhilarating.

At Sukkot there was an ex-Rugby player who was small but extremely built. I could definitely tell that he knew how to hit someone if he wanted to. My dad told me a story about when he went overseas for a game in Europe, and he saw some rugby players. The players would call the American football players sissies because they wore pads when they played. My dad told me, "Yeah, they were calling us sissies, but I told them I'd show them a sissy." He didn't tackle them or anything, but he just wanted them to know he was tough too. I'd like to see any of those players say they could have played with the likes of Lawrence Taylor, Ray Lewis, or my dad. I'm sure many great players could stop the Europeans from referring to American football players as sissies again.

Because one of the ideas of the Feast of Tabernacles is that a person is to live outside in a tent, or a temporary dwelling, we would not be set up at a five-star hotel. Most people slept in tents, but we rented an RV when we arrived. I don't think God would be too displeased with us. I know my dad sure didn't show any signs of it being a problem; we were still technically "camping out."

We arrived late at night on one of the first days of Sukkot, a bit later than others. Monte Judah, the organizer of these festivities, was a perfect Santa Claus without the overly huge belly. He was a Messianic Jew, believer in the Jewish faith while still holding that Jesus is the Christ. Of course, he and his ministry did not believe that Jesus was the name of the Messiah. His reason is fairly simple. The letter "J" did not exist in the Messiah's time; it was introduced in the seventeenth century. Also, the name for Jesus is strongly connected with the word Zeus. In the Spanish language, Jesus' name is Hesus. There is much debate on whether Jesus stemmed from Zeus, but the way the word sounds in comparison to Zeus is easy to see. Also, the Messiah's name does not have any meaning unless it is put in Hebrew as Yeshua. *Yeshua* in Hebrew means "salvation," and when used fully it is *Yahoshua,* which means "The Lord is our Salvation." Simply put, only Yeshua, or Yahoshua in Hebrew bears any meaning.

Sukkot was a blessing in disguise for me. I had gone with my parents because I was supposed to, but I hadn't a clue about any of the kids there, how they acted, or how they did things. Before arriving, I could only think about was all the attention I was going to receive from all these kids my age because of the simple fact that my dad was Reggie White. There would be no avoiding it here. Unlike school, Dad would be around. And he was fairly easy to spot. Man, was I wrong.

The first night in worship I saw something I had recently seen that summer, but had never taken part in. Hebrews dancing in a circle. I decided to dance with them. Because I was not raised Jewish and had never been exposed to this type of celebration until Dad started deeply studying the Old Testament, I had no understanding of the dances. I would just learn as I fumbled over my own feet trying to keep the rhythm. I picked up on the dances quicker than I thought. And this was the first time I absolutely enjoyed worship. After 15 years of sermons and worship and Christian schools, I finally felt the euphoria of God.

When the dancing was over I was sad. I thought it would be preaching as usual. But all the sermons would be a blessing for me. This worshiping was more interactive than my previous church or worship experience. Maybe my affinity for video games inspired this appreciation; but I found the worship involved me to the point that I enjoyed it. It wasn't just singing; it was dancing. And it wasn't just dancing; it was dancing with my friends who believed the same way I did. This was such a blessing for me, because I had felt that Dad was stifling me with his beliefs. If others believed in God and believed the sole way to go to heaven was to believe in Jesus Christ as their Lord and Savior and to obey Him, this was no longer good enough for me. I had moved up a level. I was alone. I was attending a school that didn't agree with my beliefs, even if fundamentally they were the same. I was mocked and ridiculed daily. But here, at the Feast of Tabernacles, I was no longer alone. And it helped at home: I was not as resentful toward my dad for teaching me these things, making me feel so alone in my walk with God. In Oklahoma, I knew that I was not alone, and every time I danced with these people I felt at peace.

I met a lot of great people. These people believed the same as I did and gave me a reason to keep my faith and to not back down from it no matter what. The youth leader, Brent Avery, is an extremely nice guy who is all about God. It was refreshing to meet someone who believed the same way my dad was raising me to believe. I trusted what he said. To this point, my dad taught me; so for Mr. Avery to teach and believe the same as my dad, yet coming from someone else, it was a breath of fresh air.

Over the next few days, interesting things happened. Since there was a tradition that the men cooked for the women during this time of celebration, whether through Jewish tradition or just Monte Judah's church tradition, the fact still remained, all the men in the camp would take a day out and cook. A 6-foot-5, 300-pound black man complete with a chef hat and apron, that was my dad. Because there were enough men at the festival, the same men didn't have to cook every day. The only person cooking each day was Monte Judah. Each day, 200 people were fed by seven to ten cooks. What I liked about Mr. Judah is he wasn't starstruck by my dad. He put Dad on dessert duty. There was one time Mr. Judah asked me how it felt to have my dad on a cup (a University of Tennessee cup with my dad's face on it) and I told him it was just normal to me. He didn't ask any other questions. What you see is what you get. He is a genuine guy.

Thankfully, he only had my dad making pudding. Cooking for 200 people may not have been the best way to showcase his talents. He made a living man-handling people, not preparing filet mignon. The pudding was good, though, and I told him. But there is an image of my father emblazoned on my memory, seeing this big guy with a chef's hat and apron on, serving the masses pudding. He loved every minute of it too. That's just the kind of guy he was, always willing to help out and no job was too small.

Early on, the youth decided to play football, on a partial grass, partial gravel field. All the boys were playing together, and for some reason we decided to play tackle. The ex-rugby player was short, but you wouldn't want to mess with him. The man wore a kilt, and all I kept thinking about him tackling me is that I would get killed. I do remember getting slammed into the ground, and my head bouncing off the turf. I don't remember who hit me; but I remember I had the ball and then I got one of the hardest tackles I ever had in my whole life. After I got up I had a headache. So much for people thinking I could be a football player because my dad played. I retired soon thereafter.

Later that day, some of the youth were just shooting the basketball around when one guy asked me if I could dunk. I told them I couldn't. Another guy, who was huge but only a year older than I, had an idea. He would get on all fours, and I should jump off his back to dunk the ball. He assured me, "Nah, nah, you won't hurt me, just jump off my back."

I had never done anything so stupid, but I decided to give it a try. I ran about five steps toward the guy's back, put one foot on his back, and jumped up, afraid I wasn't going to make it. With both hands, I jammed it in the hoop. The mistake I made was not grabbing onto the hoop after the dunk. I just let myself drop from five feet, landing directly on my left foot. I was on the ground immediately, almost crying. My left foot was shaking so much someone would have thought it was having a seizure. Monte Judah's son said, "Dude, that's broken." I looked up at him and said firmly, "No, it's not!" They helped me up, and while I tried to be macho and walk back to the RV, I couldn't. The guy I jumped off helped me into the RV. I just laid down on the couch. I took off my shoe. My foot had swollen up so much it looked like a plum was growing off its side.

After a rough night of sleeping, Ms. Bonita came, pulled back my covers, and immediately said to my mom, "His foot is purple!" Apparently, it being purple was a good thing; at least the blood was trying to get out and it was starting to heal up. But for the first time in my life I was enjoying worship at church, and now I couldn't even go dance with everyone because I had screwed up my foot. That was a strange twist. Soon, some of the elders of the ministry came to pray for me a prayer I had never experienced before. After putting oil on my injury they put a prayer shawl over my foot. They prayed for my foot, and I thanked them. My dad was sympathetic to me only until he found out how it happened. He kept saying, "You jumped off someone's back?!" I tried to reason with him that I had made the shot. He said, "But son, I thought I raised you with a little more sense. I don't feel sorry for you no more. I felt bad for you when I heard you sprained your ankle, but not after hearing how dumb you were in spraining it. Goodness." He didn't say this in a mean tone, but goofy, mimicking how goofy he thought I had been. It was funny even then.

I was dancing in a day and a half. Not to say that it wasn't hard, but I was dancing. My foot was still jacked up, but I was so determined to dance that I didn't let a sprained ankle bother me. Right before his sermon, Mr. Judah said, "I saw you out there dancing, Jeremy. You have a sprained ankle, right? Nah, be healed. God is good." I'm not going to say I was fully healed, but I was able to get up when I shouldn't have. That could be seen as determination or strong will, but I'm sure God appreciated what I was trying to do, and He might have eased the sprain a bit.

On the last night, the youth pulled an all-nighter. My sister and I could not stay the entire night because we had to catch our flight back home to North Carolina early the next morning. But the memories of that night would be ones to remember. We ordered pizza and just started acting crazy. One guy came up with a song before the pizza came, singing, "Oh, wouldn't it be nice if the pizza could come and the pepperoni wouldn't be pork, so we could eat it all." And everyone was just joining in and singing along. It was complete randomness, but we were all bonding. Later, we performed a star-lift where each person was lifted up by six guys to have the illusion that he was suspended in the air to look at the stars. There was a rule that no one could talk while this was going on, so each could have his own personal moment, no interruptions. For the whole ten seconds I was suspended, feeling weightless was something dear to me. It was amazing how God created those stars and everything around them. That would end Sukkot for me, and it was a sad time. As has been so true throughout my life, the bad thing about meeting a lot of people is that the more people you meet, the more goodbyes you have to say.

I went back to school with the agony of a swollen foot. My mom was fervent about me taking crutches to school. I was quickly distracted, though, when my friend, Katy Wolyniak was happy to see I had followed her advice to grow out my hair. When I first met Katy I was suspicious because she looked particularly laid back. Katy would become a great friend to me, always willing to understand why I did or didn't do certain things. She was a solid friend, and I needed one at Southshore. We would have each other's back in the year to come.

The time came to get my mind ready for basketball. Because the school was small, anyone who wanted to play could play. Even our foreign exchange student who wanted to play but hadn't played basketball was able to make the team.

Before the first practice, I decided to shoot some in the gym without any shoes. Don't ask me why I decided to do this, but I was just in my socks. I was playing around a little bit, moving slowly because my ankle was still healing, and I jumped up to get a rebound and came down on my friend's foot, spraining my right foot again. Exactly four weeks, to the very day, since the last sprain I came down and laid out on the ground. I just kept repeating, "I'm sorry, I'm sorry." I felt bad because my chiropractor told me to stay off of it, and I didn't want him to be disappointed with me when he saw me again.

As I iced my foot, I called my dad and told him I sprained it again. I thought he was going to be disappointed with me, but he told me he'd come pick me up. My chiropractor surprised me because he gave me a freezer pack to put over it and take home. No lecture. No disappointing looks.

My aunt called and said, "Jeremy! You sprained it again? You didn't really want to play basketball anyway, did you?" I told her I didn't, and she knew. I was torn on that issue. I wanted to play to have fun, but I didn't want to work hard at it. My heart wasn't in it. I felt a lot of pressure from the upper faculty and some of the students. Because I was the son of Reggie White I must be athletic, and to top it off, I'm black. The only black male in the high school must be athletic. Not me. I would give you heart and hard work. Talent? Not much. And finally, I'll do what I'm told, but I hate to be yelled at.

That next day I woke up feeling like complete crap. I went to the doctor to find out I had vertigo. The room swirled back and forth and my body felt like it too. Every time I got up or tried to move around I felt like I needed to throw up. To be certain, the doctor checked for mononucleosis. Thankfully, I didn't have it. But due to the vertigo I couldn't move around much without throwing up, my sprained foot inhibited what movement I had, and I felt the worst I'd ever felt in my life. With all this, a person would think I was happy to get a few days off from school. Not me, no sir. I was trying to get healed up to go back, because schoolwork was no joke. The requirements for biology alone were enough to make me suffer through. The biology policy was if I missed a lab, I had to complete it the next Monday I was back after school. Sick or not, I didn't want to hang around extra hours *after* school for anybody.

I tried to tell my dad how I had to get back to school. He laughed, "You're trying to go back to school? Son, when I was your age, if this were me, I would try to squeeze that out for two weeks." I told him I couldn't do it, and I'm sure he respected me for it. He just wanted me to rest. He was teasing me, but I knew my health was more important to him than a biology lab.

I made my way back to school a week later. When I returned it was the most accepted I would ever feel from everyone for the rest of the school year. Everyone was saying, "Jeremy, hey, you're back." And I felt loved. But this would be short lived, because I decided to play basketball.

I was late to the first day of practice because I had to stay after for the biology lab. Except for the first practice, the time I spent playing basketball that season at Southshore was complete hell. I hated every minute of it. I was intimidated every minute of it. I was confused, and I was being treated disrespectfully. I didn't like my coaches, I didn't like all but one of my teammates, and they didn't like me. Just coming out of vertigo and healing from an ankle injury,

I was being yelled at mercilessly. While many high school coaches yell, this was worse because I was being yelled at like I had been slacking. I could also take the orders better if I didn't feel like the whole team, save one person, was against me. Only one boy, Josh, was kind to me. Josh was home schooled, but he went to Southshore Church. Since he was a 12th grader, and Southshore didn't have a 12th grade yet, Josh was allowed to play on the school team.

Every time I would make a mistake I would get yelled at in this nasty, rather un-Christian-like way. Every time I did something wrong, my teammates took it upon themselves to scold me. I thought they were against me and didn't want me on the team. And the coach did nothing to discourage it. They had been together since grade school; and since I wasn't as good at basketball as they had stereotyped me, I was of no use to them. I know they were scared of what the coach would do to the whole team if I messed up; but when some of them messed up, they never came down on each other as hard as they did me.

In one game we were facing a team I knew we were going to beat, and I was feeling fine. When we finished with warmups and were just shooting around, I decided to do a 360 in the air and then shoot the ball from the air. The whole team jumped on me and said, "No, no, no, don't do that; don't do that!" as if I were about to hurt someone. They were so worried about what the coach would think that they didn't allow their true selves to come forth when they were practicing. We beat the team 73-27. Our assistant coach, who took over for a period while our head coach was out of the country, said that we should not have let the other team score that many points. I was amazed. He just wanted something to complain about. We ran up the score and dominated the team. A win is a win, no matter if it's by one or 100 points. I couldn't believe he said that.

The following week after practice we ran suicides. We ran what was called a 17: each player ran back to each sideline of the court, touching the line. Each line touch counted as one, and we had to do 17 of these in one minute, 12 seconds. On our third one Coach told us that we either all completed it or had to do another one. I completed both of them with at least seven seconds to spare on each one. I completed it just as hard, never letting up. One player missed it by a second, and Coach told us to line up. I literally started to cry. I told my coach I couldn't do anymore, and my legs started shaking because two hours of practice had just about finished me. He let me jog the next one, but he saw I really couldn't do it. Still, none of my teammates yelled at the guy who didn't make it.

At halftime in the locker room during another game, one particular player smelled rather badly. When this boy passed the principal, who also happened to be another player's father, the principal said, "Wooo hooo," and fanned his nose. Some of the players had already made fun of his smell; and I'm sure the principal knew this, since he had a son on the team. The principal did not make any reference to anyone else stinking. A principal, especially of a Christian school, should not be demean anyone, especially a child. If he had joked, "Man, you guys were playing hard, and I can smell it," that may have been funny. But the fact that he singled out one innocent kid wasn't Christ like; and Christians are supposed to be Christ like.

Every day I dreaded every minute of practice. Games I could handle, but the coach told the whole team to not save anything for the fourth quarter, but to give our all every quarter. One game in particular, a guy on the other team lobbed a pass halfway down the court, and our guy didn't flinch when he could have easily jumped up and deflected or intercepted it. Granted, he was turned around not facing the ball, but a player must be aware of what's going on. My teammate was by our bench and could hear us telling him about the pass, but he wasn't disturbed after he missed the opportunity. I couldn't understand it. If that had been me, again, I would have been bawled out.

My parents both knew about my basketball troubles, and, because I confided in my mom, she knew I wanted to stop playing. I didn't really want to quit, because I don't like quitting, but I was miserable. When a kid plays a sport, ultimately it is to have fun, even through the tough work-outs. But I wasn't having any fun. I was dejected and didn't want to be around those guys. I was intimidated too, because of the vibes I was getting from them when they wouldn't even speak to me except to yell at me or tell me what I did wrong. There was no, "good job, keep it up," from my teammates when I was doing something right. From years of watching my dad, and from playing recreational basketball myself, I know that's what teammates should do. The closer the team is, the better off they usually are. And if the team isn't winning, at least the players are having fun, working hard together. Finally, one day when I was supposed to go to practice, I told my dad I didn't want to go. For the first time in my life, my dad had already discussed his concerns with the coach. He purposefully didn't step in, until now, when he found my treatment extreme. I had talked to Mom earlier, and as my dad came into her office, she said, "Reggie, what do you think?" He said, "Well, if you're not enjoying it, don't do it."

And that was that. I felt so free that day. I didn't show up to practice. I just didn't go. I was so exhilarated. Everything seemed to be right in the world. The color in my room seemed to brighten and the red digital time on my clock seemed more vibrant. Things were looking up.

But when I went to school the next day, one of my teammates pointed out to me that I didn't show up to practice, like I didn't know. A week later when the coach got back from his vacation he called me into his office. I knew immediately what it was about. He jumped right into it. "So, I get back from out of town, and I heard that you quit." I told him I did. He said, "Well, you know you are not a good basketball player, but I like your character the most, and I want you to be on the team because of that." I said some words, listened to him some more, and knew from the second I walked in there that I was not going back to that wretched basketball team. I use the term team loosely.

Whether or not the coach agreed with me, I had been vindicated. My dad had already been willing to take me out of Southshore at midyear because of the physical stress it was causing me. I told him I could stick it out for the rest of the year. Just like the two weeks with vertigo when I was trying to get back into school, Dad admired my sense of responsibility. But he shouldn't have been surprised; where did he think I learned it? Dad never just quit anything. Yeah, he made career moves, but he never left anyone in the lurch. And I endured all I could on that basketball team, to the detriment of my physical health and mental well being. When Dad said it was enough, then it was enough.

I told one family that I had quit, and the wife said to me, "No, you didn't quit. Quitting implies that you are on a team, and you were not on a team with those boys." I agreed with her, and I appreciated that she noticed. That was the end of my basketball career at Southshore. Somehow my mom was able to pull strings to get me on the recreational league team I had played on the year before. And that would restore my fun in basketball.

That season was great. Since I jumped on the team, I had almost stacked the team a little because of my height and my will to play. We also had the best player in the league, and we all worked well together. The player who beat my team the previous year in the championship was on my team. I knew for a fact we were going to win the championship this year. We had good team chemistry, and we did play in the championship game. But this year, I could not play in it because I was unable to get off from work.

Originally our assistant coach told us we were going to play the championship game on a Sunday, but the date was changed to Saturday. This was a problem, because I found out that Saturday morning. Literally about an hour and a half before I was supposed to show up for work, the date was changed. I couldn't call in to say I wouldn't be in. It wasn't a regular type of job.

In the early part of 2002, I became employed as a kennel worker for a veterinarian, because at that time I wanted to be a veterinarian. I loved animals. To have a job that I was working around the veterinarians and interacting with all those dogs and cats was like heaven to me. Well … it was like that before I actually was on the job for a time. Employees were assigned to walk the dogs on certain days; and on the weekends, there two people were scheduled to walk and feed the dogs. Those were the only two employees scheduled at the veterinarian office on weekends. As I was one of those people on the day of the championship game, I couldn't call and say I couldn't come in because other people might not have been available either. And to top it off, if only one person was available to walk and feed those dogs on top of cleaning their cages, it would have been unfair. I know many teenagers would have called in anyway, but I couldn't. I couldn't let them down. It was my job. Ugh.

The game I knew we were going to be in all year was in hours, and I couldn't play in it. To make matters worse, when I got back from work, my cousin, Wesley, had played and won his lower-aged league championship game, and my sister told me we lost, taking second place again. My cousin, who likes to rub things in and insti-gate, said the most annoying things because he won his champi-onship tournament. He kept asking me, "What's the difference between our medals?" "Why is yours red and mine has blue on it?" "Did you win your game?" I put up with it. He knew exactly what he was doing, and I couldn't do anything about it.

I did find some happiness at home even after all of the hard times in basketball, particularly at Southshore. I played a game called "Phantasy Star Online," a role-playing game with the main objective to make the character stronger. I could connect to the Internet through the game system and play with three other people online. It was fun because people would start to become friends. With a keyboard for the system, I could type to them to let them know I was in trouble or what I needed as a weapon, and some were gracious enough to give great weapons.

The only problem with this game was there were thieves. Obviously they were not breaking the law, but it was still the princi-ple of it. If it was mine, it was mine. I got stolen from a lot, because when I "died" and dropped my items, someone picked them up. Either my teammate could revive me, leave me there, or in the case of thieves, take my stuff. The only way I found around this was to be friends with people who knew how to hack into other people's systems. One time when I was stolen from, I told my friend online about it, and he called his people and they found the thief, made his screen go black, and he lost all of the weapons and money that he had. This game was a good outlet after a bad day. And if I may convey my attitude toward the people who do steal on Internet games and who cheat, stop. That is all.

The treatment at Southshore grew worse, including daily bitter remarks as one kid confirmed. When I said I was an outcast, he said straight to my face, "Yeah, you are." Through all of that, my solid group of friends, Katy Wolyniak, Lauren Fuselier, and Mandi Grimes stood strong in support. All of the girls were different, yet they all were the same. They respected people who deserved it, and they treated people kindly who treated them kindly. They were not snotty, and they had a good sense of humor. Mandi, in particular, could boast one of the highest GPAs in the tenth grade class. The girl is smart. We always sat together during lunch and talked about random things, meaningful things, and Bible things. We also talked about how mean and horrible many of our fellow classmates were. We didn't go around saying mean things to others, but we vented to each other and helped each other make it out of there without too much pain. They were my friends for who I am, not whose son I was. They encouraged me when others despised me for unspoken reasons. One thing we agreed on that we appreciated was our math teacher, Mrs. Clark.

Mrs. Clark, my geometry teacher was somewhat of an acquired taste, because she would push you to do your best and behave while doing it. But she cared about all of her students. Early in the year I had to stay after class with three other students, because in class, I was talking when I wasn't supposed to be. When she taught, she taught, and when she joked, she joked. Students would have to learn that about her and realize when to do and when not to do things. I never got in any kind of trouble with her after that.

We also particularly liked Bible class. Although we were all in different classes, we liked our teacher's attitude when it came to God's Word. Even if he said things we didn't agree with, he heard our point of view and respected it. Also, he did not try to drill any of his beliefs into us. He was a great Bible teacher because he would

Lauren Fuselier (left) and Mandi Grimes (not pictured), two of my best friends, followed me to Hopewell High School.

explain things, but still open it up for discussion and respect others' viewpoints on the scripture passage.

Invariably, every teacher will occasionally need a substitute. On that day in class, somebody brought up the fact that I don't eat certain types of meat, more specifically, that I keep the food commandments in the Old Testament. One girl then asked me, "So, you don't believe any of the words of Paul?" Of course, I immediately got defensive. I said, "I do believe the words of Paul. What I don't believe is that he was saying that we should not follow the food laws anymore." Someone else immediately brought up Acts 10. The same scripture passage that Tim earlier in the year brought up with me was not about to corner me twice; I knew my stuff.

I explained to her that the whole story was about Peter not being prejudiced against Cornelius. I went through it with the whole class, verse by verse. Animals, when mentioned in Acts 10, were used as a metaphor to explain something to Peter at the time. This metaphor had nothing to do literally with food. Whenever people believe we do not have to keep the food laws mentioned in Leviticus 11 and Deuteronomy 14 because of this chapter in Acts, they need to turn to the passage. Acts 10:9 states, "About noon the following day as they were on their journey and approaching the city, Peter went up on the roof to pray. (10) He became hungry and wanted something to eat, and while the meal was being prepared, he fell into a trance. (11) He saw heaven opened and something like a large sheet being let down to earth by its four corners. (12) It contained all kinds of four-footed animals, as well as reptiles of the earth and birds of the air. (13) Then a voice told him, 'Get up, Peter. Kill and eat.' (14) 'Surely not, Lord!' Peter replied, 'I have never eaten anything impure or unclean.' (15) The voice spoke to him a second time, 'Do not call anything impure that God has made clean.'"

This is the part at which most people stop, saying that God made all things clean, but read on. Skip down to verse 17, "While Peter was wondering about the meaning of the vision, the men sent by Cornelius found out where Simon's house was and stopped at the gate. (18) They called out, asking if Simon who was known as Peter was staying here." Now, this is the most important part because one cannot interpret the Bible, the Bible must interpret itself, and it clearly states in verse 19, "While Peter was still thinking about the vision, the Spirit said to him, 'Simon, three men are looking for you. (20) So get up and go downstairs. Do not hesitate to go with them, for I have sent them."

As we can see, while he was pondering on the vision, God sent men to his house, but not just any men, Gentiles. Jews were not allowed to associate with Gentiles. In verse 28, Peter clearly states, "You are well aware that it is against our law for a Jew to associate with a Gentile or visit him. But God has shown me that I should not call any man impure or unclean." Right there. God's whole vision to Peter was to use a metaphor, which was unclean foods, for him to understand that he should not judge people just because they are not Jewish. God had taken something Peter had grown up with—keeping kosher—to explain to him that he should not be prejudice to the Gentiles who came to his door. There is no other explanation as clear as that, and there is no way the passage is about food. Peter was wondering what the vision could mean; if it meant he didn't have to keep the food laws anymore then he would have come to that conclusion within the text. But it is never mentioned. Still many ministers, preachers, pastors and Christians believe they have a license to eat at will, when the Bible doesn't say that at all.

At lunch time, as I was ending my discussion, I looked up to find the substitute teacher intrigued. I had accomplished something. I had finally defended a point that I needed to continue in my own belief. To explain it to a classroom of 20-some people was an accomplishment, because I was only 15, and I was just a baby with it at the time. But for the first time I felt like a man in my beliefs. I knew what I had to do and why I had to do it. I had arrived; I was not a self-proclaimed Christian who couldn't defend the reason for the belief.

I got out of the Bible club, because it seemed like people were more interested in arguing about the belief of predestination rather than discussing the Bible maturely. I went instead to Buddy club, which was fun because I like kids. Four other girls and I—because no other guys signed up for it—went to the second grade to help them out with little projects, homework or whatever. The kids were so excited to see me, and it was simply because I was a guy. Later, I would notice in day cares and early education, there aren't many male workers. I do like to volunteer with kids, although my career plan now is in journalism.

In January, when I was expecting to be off for Martin Luther King Jr. holiday, I found out that Southshore did not take that day off. Skipping school would have caused more disruption in making up the classwork. Many old friends of mine couldn't believe it. I asked the reasoning for this at school, and I was told that they did not want to uplift one man. Southshore considered themselves a Christian school but they would not try to indoctrinate a person but rather teach Christian values and the Bible. But while in English class we were learning about John Calvin and Calvinism. The school's program pushed Presbyterian Calvinistic beliefs upon us. Ultimately, they will uplift a single man named Calvin, but not a man who changed the face of the civil rights movement in America. Martin Luther King Jr. and Calvin played two entirely different roles. It is not wrong to recognize a man for advocating peace in the name of what is morally right. But it is wrong to uplift a man on a specific doctrine if you say that you are a Calvinist or a Lutheran. Paul's writings state that he told the people not to say, "I follow Paul," but to be followers of the Lord. When we start glorifying one man, we forget who gave that man life and who gave that man the word he claims to be given. As believers it is our responsibility to put God ahead of everyone else and say we follow God, not one specific person.

One fun time was at Mandi and Lauren's party. At this point my hair was long enough to put into twists. Everyone was dressed up, and I didn't know I was supposed to dress up. So I buttoned up my baseball jersey and walked in. The greatest thing that night is when I asked the DJ to play some Michael Jackson. As the music came on, I started dancing and everyone was pretty amazed by my moves. Granted the floor wasn't slick, so I couldn't do some of the moves as well as I wanted to. Nonetheless, I still made the crowd of people who were watching me go wild. At that party was a girl I liked. When we were sitting on the couch as the party was ending she put her leg up to rest it on my leg, almost like a footstool. Later, I found out that she was doing it to make another guy jealous. And I actually wrote her a poem telling her how much I liked her. Looking back, it wasn't that much. I know older people can relate when I say that I don't know what I was thinking liking certain people when I was younger. I know why I did. I didn't have a wide selection because it was such a small school.

As spring break approached, my dad mentioned that we would take the RV back to Oklahoma. This time Dad had business, and we went to visit some friends. Also, we took two family friends, Greg and Joy Briggs. After a 22-hour drive in an RV, I was bored in every sense of the word. To top it off, it was the Feast of Unleavened Bread, and we couldn't eat any yeast the whole week. I had just participated in Passover the week before, and I was a sight trying to keep a yarmulke on my head with a hairpin. Everyone was asked to wear one at the event we attended, but it wasn't required. I did it out of respect. Overall, Oklahoma was the worst spring break ever. All I did was stay at our friends' house, avoid all yeast, and play a basketball video game all day, literally. My dad told me, "Next year we'll do something fun." But truthfully, I didn't want to do anything with him. I wanted to do something fun, but alone with my friends. I was getting to that age that I was ready to be out of the house.

On the way back from Oklahoma, my dad and Ms. Joy debated about the Bible. My dad was saying that someone could serve another God without knowing it. Mrs. Joy disagreed, saying if someone were naïve to a particular statue in their house having an idolistic past, then they were not giving themselves to that idol in a worshiping manner. My dad cited a verse in Jeremiah that reads, "The heart is exceedingly wicked," and he went on to say the heart will deceive a person, and the person will not know he is worshiping something. Mrs. Joy disagreed with that. When my dad believed in something, he stuck to it. Later, he would pull back a little from this statement and not be too picky about the heart "deceiving" a person without the person's awareness, but he was still doing this out of reverence to God and trying to be the best person he could be for the Lord.

After basketball season I decided to take up another sport. Every Saturday for about two months, I was in a bowling league. And I stunk. At first I stunk because I was trying to put a curve on the ball with only two fingers in the holes. The coach told me not to try, because I didn't have any control. I started to bowl straight for a while. One game I got a decent score. And because my handicap was so high, our team moved into first place. About three weeks later, with no warning, I was able to put a spin on the ball. A guy on another team almost bowled a perfect game, but on the very last frame he knocked down only nine. He went on to spare that one and get another strike afterward. Everyone in the alley clapped for him. I had never seen anything like it in my life. It was something amazing to witness. Most people thought it was funny that I bowled, because looking at my dad one would never think he bowled, but he did bowl occasionally. It was a funny sight to see. He would actually palm the bowling ball and chuck it down the lane. He wasn't too bad a bowler at all.

With the year coming to a close, I wanted to get out of Southshore and go to a public school. I asked my mom about it, and she said those infamous words, "We'll see." All that meant is that we had to talk to Dad. On the way home from school one day she said, "OK, let's all talk about whether Jeremy should go to public school or not." My dad was whistling to a song, then stopped, like the scratch of a vinyl record. He then said, "That's fine."

And that was the end of it. My mom looked back at me, and I looked at her, and we were both shocked to see him react so fast. It was as if he was making a decision about where to eat on a Sunday afternoon. That sealed my deal. And my sister's too.

When I told Mandi, Lauren, and Katy, they were all happy for me. All three of them wanted out too. But Katy decided she couldn't, because she was so close to graduating and it wouldn't look good if she switched to another school for her senior year. Mandi and Lauren, on the other hand, still had to talk to their parents, but they were going for it. Mandi wanted to see if she could maintain as strong a GPA in a public school. It wasn't that she couldn't handle it, but she wanted all of her credits and her 5.33 GPA to transfer.

When Mandi talked to her parents, her dad was the deciding factor for her as well. He said it was fine, and soon Lauren said she was going to public school too. All of us were happy.

Mrs. Clark took me in the hall during one geometry class to ask me if I was leaving, and I told her yes. She immediately threw a fit because she liked me. Mr. Nerness found out through someone else, and he wanted me to stay, too. Also our Spanish teacher loved us. Other than those three teachers, no one seemed to care. When Mandi's dad called the school to tell them she was leaving, he had to leave a message. No one called him back to ask why. It seems strange that a school dedicated to Christ and Christ-like attributes didn't call to inquire why one of their best academically, well behaved, strong-in-the-Lord students was leaving.

The only response I received was from a guidance counselor who asked my mom why I was leaving. My mom explained that I didn't feel welcomed there, and that I wasn't being treated well by the other students. The counselor told my mom that as Christians we have to suffer sometimes; my mom asked her why I had to be the one who was suffering, especially in high school. She felt I should have a good experience, and the ironic thing was, I was on a different level than the other kids when it came to the Bible. I can say that with no big ego, because I know it's true. I saw it when we talked about the Bible, and I saw it in their responses. And yet my mom was being told that I needed to be the one suffering. That didn't go over so well with my mom.

On the last day of exams, as Lauren, Mandi, and I walked out of Southshore, our beloved Spanish teacher saw us leaving. Later, she told Lauren that it was almost surreal in the way we were leaving, with the light hitting the door, as if to say, "There go the last few decent students at this school." There was a comfort for those parents to make that decision once my dad did. If Reggie White, whose beliefs were held in high regard in the community, felt strong about pulling out of a Christian school, they could too.

The summer between my tenth and eleventh grade year I went to the summer camp "Camp Yeshua." *Yeshua* is the name of Jesus in Hebrew. The only thing about this camp that stunk was the trip back to Oklahoma. When we arrived we were late. I hated walking in late, especially with my father (causing a scene), around my friends and peers. I didn't want everyone to know automatically that my dad was Reggie White. I didn't want them to assume things before they got to know me. But if I had known anything at all about the people I was about to meet I wouldn't have worried about it.

But at the time I did. And I copped a terrible attitude. When we walked into the building, I saw two familiar faces, Joe and Andy Pierre, my friends from Green Bay. Any other time I would have been ecstatic, but I had an attitude, and I didn't like to be surprised. My dad told me, "You better straighten up; and lose the attitude. This is supposed to be a vacation for you." I was so angry because he and Mom kept teasing how they might come and stay at the camp with us. I knew they were joking, but I just wished they would stop. They were taking it a bit too far. I'm sure the unending drive to Oklahoma didn't help.

As camp started, I realized just how busy I would be. It wasn't a vacation per se, because we awoke early in the morning with planned activities the entire day. One of the afternoon activities was to experiment in crafts and hobbies. I decided to join the guitar group, but I realized that a little guitar knowledge would help. I switched to a balloon animal-making class. I had a lot more fun in that.

This camp felt a lot like the Feast of Tabernacles back in October. Many of the same people were at the camp. One night we played a game in which the object of the game was to get three people who believed in God to a central location outside of the building. The only thing was, some of us were deemed non-believers with the "mark of the beast" on us, and it was our job to lie and say we were believers. When we got three people in a group we would get a camp leader, and if one person in the group was a non-believer, we couldn't move on. For about 30 minutes I was able to lie like crazy because it was part of the game. I had the "mark of the beast." My job was to ruin the believers and hope they didn't get to the main location. The game was also played at night, which added to the fun. While the moral was maybe not everyone is how he seems, I discovered all of the people in my group had the mark of the beast: we were all lying to each other.

We also all went to a rope course. We could walk on thin rope, while having aid to hold us up if we were to fall. But I didn't do that. I did the climbing wall. It takes a powerful upper body to complete the climbing wall solo. For me, it took five people on the ground, pulling my rope to help me to the top. Once at the top, I was able to zip line down to the ground. I took a running start and jumped off of the ledge. I zipped my way to the ground for an exhilarating ten seconds.

On the last day, Brent, who was also our youth leader at the Feast of Tabernacles, took us hiking on the mountainside. It took us about 20 minutes to climb up the distance to the spot where we would reside for his teaching. It was a beautiful sight over the horizon. After the sermon, because we were all tired and hot, we went on back down the mountain. To see the big rock on which we had just been sitting gave us a sense of accomplishment. When it was time for us to leave, I wasn't happy; no one was. We had all bonded so closely that week we did not want to leave each other. I didn't know when I was going to see some of those people again, but I had great memories.

From camp I was to go to Green Bay with Joe and Andy. But before we got there we stayed in Oklahoma at our friends' house. We managed in a short time to get in a great deal of trouble. We thought it would be cool to get in the trunk of our friend's Mercedes. First I got in, closed the lid on top, and curled up in the darkness. There was a safety button inside for potentially trapped people. I got out without a hitch, and Joe decided to try it. He chose a different Mercedes, whose trunk was a lot smaller. He took some golf clubs out and got right in, with little room to spare. After five seconds he said, "OK, guys, let me out." Even with the keys to the car the trunk wouldn't open. I assured Joe we were working on it. He said, "Guys…guys…what's going on, guys?" We tried to remain calm and said, "Joe, it won't open. We can't get you out." Joe started to panic. Later he told me he started to think about all the wrong things he had done in his life, and he figured this was all his sins catching up with him.

Bill and Stacy Horn, who owned the Mercedes, came out to see what was going on. His son didn't say anything; he just let Joe's muffled words from the trunk do the talking. Mr. Horn's face was priceless when it registered that an 18-year-old (his son) and two 15-year-olds (Andy and me) had a 16-year-old (Joe) stuck in his trunk. Mr. Horn got the keys from his son and tried to open the trunk. Like we hadn't. It wasn't working. He tried again, and it popped open. Joe popped out of the car so quickly that I grabbed him and hugged him like I hadn't seen him in the longest time. I had panicked and couldn't imagine what would happen if we couldn't get him out. "All I felt was this life air coming to me, and I was so happy to get out of there," Joe would later tell me. Inevitably this story of stupidity got back to my dad. Instead of being mad, he laughed at us and asked how we could be so dumb. He dubbed us the "Trunk Boys," and he added this story to his repertoire for all our friends and family.

That summer I knew for certain I was going to public school, and I was excited but a little scared. I didn't know what to expect. A boy I knew who already went to the school showed me the yearbook, and I found a girl in there who I thought was cute. At least that gave me some sort of reason to go. And that reason was to see if there were any other cute girls. As that summer came to a close, I was starting a new part of my life, public school. Hopewell.

10

Hopewell High School, in Huntersville, North Carolina, is where I would spend the remainder of my high school years. As a junior I was about to see the finish line. Sitting on a wall inside the school front in the first few days, I was still a bit paranoid as people were passing me, because I didn't know if they knew who I was or not. Some of them looked and pointed, and others just looked. I wasn't sure if they were thinking, *Who's that new kid?* or wondering if I was Reggie White's son. Later, I found I mostly was correct that they knew I was Reggie White's son and that's why they had looked and pointed, but in a sea of 2,100 students, I could get lost very quickly.

I didn't know how people would react to my faith and the way I believed. I was no longer wearing the tzit tzits, partially because I didn't want people asking me all sorts of questions and partially because I might not have been wearing jeans every day to put them around my belt loops. My mom told me I had made my point at Southshore. I think she fully understood.

The very first day of school I saw her, the girl in the yearbook, coming down the hall. No lie, I thought she had a glow around her. More luck, I found I had two classes with her. Her name was Alyce (UH-LEECE) McGirt. I planned to play it cool for a while and get to know her. While there were a lot of cute girls at school, Alyce seemed to have a funny personality. I would go on to become good friends with her that year but never made a move. For my entire junior year I was just friends with her, and that was all right with me.

At my first parents' night in public school, I felt the same gut-wrenching stress I had all my life at new schools. I dreaded that night. I didn't want my dad going because I didn't want my teachers to know who I was. I didn't want them either showing me any leniency or being too strict on me because they thought I was a spoiled brat and needed to learn the value of work. My dad went anyway, and I was not too worried. We were in Huntersville, not Green Bay. Maybe so many wouldn't notice. I just took it in stride. One of the first classes that I quickly came to enjoy was AP (Advanced Placement) English Language. Mr. Todd Humphrey taught me the only AP class I took that year. Mr. Humphrey is a great guy, genuine and really wanted to help everyone learn. He reminded me of my dad in that he was passionate about his faith and he could admit when he was wrong. It was appropriate that his was the first class my father entered.

It wasn't until the next day I was outed. In English class, Mr. Humphrey said, "You know, Jeremy, I knew you were a humble young man by the way you carry yourself in class and what you say, but now I understand where you get it from. When your dad came into class I said to myself, 'I know I recognize him.' When I told him, 'My name is Todd Humphrey. What is your name?' he said, 'Reggie' and stepped back. I thought to myself, *This guy is Reggie White and he isn't saying that he used to play football or anything he just said, 'I'm Reggie.'* I thought that was so humble of him, because he could have been bragging about who he was, but he was simply Reggie."

I'm sure I was sliding under my desk at that point, but one kid spoke up and said, "Who is it you said?" And he said, "Reggie White, the NFL football player." At that point if I had been a white male instead of a black one, someone would have seen the red all over my face. Suddenly, it was hot in the room. I had just started making friends all on my own and worrying less about anyone knowing who my dad was, and boom! My teacher blew my cover. One girl looked at me from across the room, and said, "Whoa, look who's popular now." That's exactly what I didn't want.

The next day Mr. Humphrey took me into his office and said, "I was talking to my wife yesterday, and she said, 'Todd, did you ever think maybe he didn't want you to say that?' And I said, 'No I didn't.' So I just want to apologize to you. I didn't mean to put your business out there, but I was just amazed at how humble you were, and I was amazed at where you had gotten it from. That's all." I told him I fully understood. I wasn't mad at him, I was just shocked. But Mr. Humphrey became one of my favorite teachers ever. He wanted his students to love learning like he did, and he wanted everyone to know how much he valued each person. I thought that when a few people found out about me that it would spread like wildfire. It didn't at all. I was relieved and all the more glad.

As well as acceptance, I found that public school seemed to have more religious diversity and open-mindedness. There were Christians, Muslims, Jews, atheists, and some who weren't sure what they believed. I fully understood what my parents meant when they used to say, "We get along with non-Christians better than a lot of Christians." I had people ask me why I didn't eat a certain way or what I did on the Sabbath, and I would tell them with my guard up. People at Hopewell would say, "Oh, for real? That's cool." And that would be the end of it. This was new to me, because the kids at Southshore only wanted to know in order to debate me. For the most part, Hopewell kids were just curious. I hadn't felt that acceptance in a long time.

I had a new experience as a junior: I was excited to have African-American studies, but I'll admit I was taken aback when I saw Mrs. Luckadoo, a white lady, teaching it. I'm not racist, I'm not prejudice, and I'm not against it; I was just surprised and considered it ironic. Everyone in that all-black class was so chill, and we easily got along. Not to say that if there was a white person in the class that we wouldn't have gotten along; but something about sharing a commonality made us feel understood. For example, a white person in a room full of black people will gravitate to another white person. Not that race is so important that it should separate someone. Mrs. Luckadoo taught well every day; and in the end, I think we taught her some things too.

The rivalry between the Class of 2003 and the Class of 2004 caused daily excitement. The class of '03 thought they had one up on '04 because of the fact that they could make a "0" and a "3" with just one hand. We would say, "Ohhh Fooohhhh Youu Know!!!" And then they would come back with the same thing, except say " '03." At least ours rhymed. But yes, it was fun to be a part of a group without stipulations.

One morning, I went to school, wearing my dad's Panthers jersey. My history teacher who was the varsity football coach, saw it and said, "So you like Reggie White?" I said, "Yeah, I like him." He said, "You know his daughter goes to school here. If you're nice to Jecolia, you might be able to get it signed." I sat back in my chair, thinking of the irony, but only said to him, "Oh, OK, I'll have to keep that in mind." He didn't know. He thought he was giving me a good tip, and I tried to hold back a smile. Of course, later, he found out and his face flushed. He said, "You must have thought I was pretty stupid." I told him I didn't, but I did get a good laugh out of it.

I decided to continue to play in the recreational basketball league. We had a pretty decent team, plus one giant ball hog. We would lose games because he hogged the ball all the time. We never worked it around, and we could never get off a good shot because he held the ball too long. We didn't have quite the season I had been used to the previous two years; it was a lot worse. One of the last games the ball hog actually passed me the ball underneath, and I got it in the hoop for the score. He told me later in the huddle, "I never trusted getting you the ball down low; I guess it's a good thing." I was thinking to myself, *You are saying this to me at the end of the season?* My dream of going back to the championship game for the third year in a row was gone, but it was just rec ball. It was fun.

Around this time Taylor Johnson and his family moved to Charlotte from Minnesota. He and his brother Kyle would go to Hopewell with me. And as the weeks continued, I loved Hopewell. I loved going every day, and part of me dreaded going home, because school was partially my getaway from my dad. We had really started having problems with each other. Most teenage boys say they struggled with their fathers, but I know our struggle was different. Ours was mostly unspoken.

During that time, my dad was immersed in the Hebrew language. When I told him I was taking Latin, he asked me if there was a Hebrew class I could take. When I told him there wasn't, he told me there should be. He kept trying to get me to learn Hebrew, but I wanted nothing to do with it. He, my mom, and my aunt took a class together at a seminary during my first semester as a junior. He was quickly disappointed when he went, however, because he realized that the teacher wasn't presenting them any new information. He considered his time there wasted, because the class wasn't delving as deep into the Hebrew language as he wanted. My dad passed the time by joking about how my mom and aunt would talk during tests and by saying they were cheating (of course they weren't). It was funny to hear the three people who reared me now experiencing school all over again. Of course it was only one class, but still, to see them act like the Three Stooges was a sight.

My dad was disgusted to learn from where people get their modern image of a white Jesus. He told me one of the original paintings of Jesus was completed by a man who had his brother (a European) sit in as his Jesus model. My dad couldn't believe it, and he didn't want any images of his Savior for fear he might actually worship the image, or representation, rather than the being it was supposed to represent. I fully understood this, because every time I close my eyes and think of Jesus I have a white person in my head; and every time I think of God I think of an old Caucasian man with white hair, reminiscent of Zeus.

To please God he revisited a verse in the Bible that stated one shall not make a graven image. Dad took this strictly, and he decid-

ed he didn't want an image of anything in the entire house. No
Beanie Babies, no stuffed animals, no statues. Anything and everything that was fake and representing something living or once living,
he did not want in the house. My dad called a family meeting to discuss it with my mom, my sister, and me. My dad assured me, before
he called my sister and mom in the living room, that what he was
about to say would not come against me, but would disagree with
my mom and sister. With my frustration building since the days of
Pokémon's exodus, I was hoping not to react, but it was only a matter of time before I would erupt. The first spews were that night.

Because I was so mad and sad all at the same time, I couldn't
take it anymore, and I asked to go upstairs (I know, really rebellious,
huh?). He told me I couldn't, that I had to sit and listen to what he
was saying. I tried again. "Can I please go upstairs?" He bellowed, "I
said no, Jeremy." Out of nowhere I exploded behind angry tears. A
screaming voice I hardly recognized as my own said, "I need to go
upstairs." He told me, "Sit down!" I had never heard my dad get as
angry with me as he was right then. That was the first time I had
ever really openly defied him. At 15.

The tension grew unbearable, and I needed to get out of there. He
said a few more things out of frustration, and then, "I'm doing this
because I think it is what we're supposed to do to please God. That's
all I'm trying to do; that's all I'm trying to do." He took a deep breath.
"You can leave now." He stood and went to his room and closed the
door. I went upstairs and started to cry. I felt alone and helpless; but
what I didn't expect, most of all, I was torn. Here I was, the son of
Reggie White, in a house and with a status that most people would
die to be in, but I didn't like being under my father's roof. The drastic
changes we made month after month were exhausting and unending.
Every time I would get used to a new rule he would say he was
wrong or we needed to add more. Nothing would end with him, and
we were always learning new things and changing our lifestyle every
day. At any given time, I could tell anyone a new fact we learned
because my dad was always teaching us something new. Later, he
read in the Torah that bird and animal figurines are not idols.

I remember coming home from school one day to find Dad had thrown away a lot of statues. He had thrown away some of his Mackey Awards, Defensive Player of the Year, his college trophies, even my mom's trophies, and many of his gold and silver carvings of Bible characters he got in Israel. The tossed trophies were the ones with images of people on them. When I realized he was clearing out our false idols, it was just one more thing to hold inside and not tell him that I was aggravated about. As I mentioned before, my dad was rash in his decision making for the sole purpose of pleasing God. If he had found somewhere in the Bible that God said rings were idols or false gods, my dad surely would have thrown away his Super Bowl ring. But for all of the football fans out there, don't worry; he found no such verse, and the Super Bowl ring is undamaged and safe.

In December 2002, all my pent-up frustration exploded without much warning. My cousin Shari was living with us again, and sometimes it was like having another sister in the house. Close to winter break, Kyle, Taylor, Mr. Keith, my sister, Jecolia, Shari and I came home from an outing together, and Shari made a comment. Jokingly, I said, "Hush up, ho." Shari got very angry; she asked for permission to cuss me out. I didn't realize I was going to make her that angry. I shouldn't have said it, but I thought that she would take a joke.

After we got in the house she didn't want to talk to me. I tried to apologize, even when she didn't want to hear it. She finally accepted it, but she still didn't want to talk to me. The healing process started slowly. And it made an abrupt stop when my dad called me into his room. I knew it. He said, "Jeremy, did you call Shari a ho?!" I said I did. He looked at me dumbfounded. I could see the disbelief in his eyes. I told him that I was joking, and he said I didn't need to joke about such things. I thought he overreacted, and he couldn't believe I was nonchalant. Soon after the Johnsons left, Dad called everyone into the family room for a talk. I sat by my mom, wishing it was over before it started. My dad had taken his side by my sister and my cousin.

Shari looked like she was in another world, and I was just wishing I wasn't there. My dad said in a stern voice, "Jeremy, when you do things like that, that is a reflection on me. Do you know how I felt in front of Keith and his family when I heard that you said that? You need to apologize to Shari."

"Dad, I did apologize already!"

"Don't raise your voice at me." His eyes were locked onto mine.

"Dad, I'm not trying to, I'm just saying I already did it. Can I go?" My voice was rising.

He told me no. I mumbled under my breath, "Oh, God."

He cut his eyes at me, and snorted, "Oh God, what?!"

And I had had enough of it, I told him I already apologized, and I just wanted to leave. I stood. He told me to stay, and then, "OK, you apologized to her, but I want you to apologize to Mr. Keith and everyone who was in that car." I asked him why. He said since I was representing him I needed to apologize to everyone for how I acted. I told him it didn't concern them, that Shari was the only person that I needed to worry about. He told me I had no choice, that I had to do it.

That was it. I stood up and shouted, "But it doesn't concern anyone else, Dad! The only person that matters is Shari!" I think I said some other things, but I don't remember. And that's probably best. I remember screaming, almost crying, and Dad coming toward me and I was yelling in his face. From nowhere, my mom got between us, because he was yelling at me too.

At that point he was fed up because everyone in the room disagreed with him. And he said, "OK, I'm gonna leave!!"

My sister said, "Bye!" sarcastically.

He turned to her and said, "Bye? Bye!?" He came over to the couch to say something to her, and she cringed as if he had been an abusive father our whole lives, which he was not in any way. He got his keys and left.

I ran upstairs to my room and started hitting the wall in my bathroom. I just cried and cried. Mom ran up after me, crying, and Shari and Jecolia sat still on the couch, bawling wildly. I don't know if I'll ever forget my mom's cry that day; it was the cry that would make one think a family was crumbling at its roots when, of course, it wasn't. We just never had unleashed our feelings before.

Standing in my bathroom, I wanted to be in a place where no one knew I was. I hid in a closet. Because our house was so large I should be difficult to find. In the closet, I kept praying to God, asking Him why I had been taught all this Bible knowledge and why I had to be Reggie White's son. As I was praying, I heard Mr. Keith say, "Jeremy, hey, buddy, where are you?" And then I realized he had come back. I didn't want to talk to him or to anyone, but something inside me called out behind a raspy voice, "I'm in here."

He opened the door, and instead of asking me to come out, he came in with me. After a few minutes, he said, "Jeremy, you have been serving the same God since you were a little boy. The problem is, you are ready to be out of the house because you are actually two years older, maturity wise, than your age depicts."

For the first time it seemed like someone really understood what I was going through. How did he know I wondered if I were serving the same God now that we were learning all these new things? If I never learned these new things would I have gone to hell anyway? All these questions had been swimming around in my mind for the last two years, and it was painful. Even if I had a chance to answer them, my dad would bring up something else we had to do or weren't supposed to do. The constant unrest and pressure was too much.

After Mr. Keith finished talking, I went downstairs and found my dad playing one of the arcade shooting games we had in the basement. I knew he was trying to forget. I called out to him slowly, "Dad," and he dropped his head and turned off the game. I apologized for yelling at him. He turned immediately for me. When he locked me in a hug, he started crying and told me he was sorry too. Later, I would be forced to tell him what exactly was bothering me. He actually grounded me until I started talking. I didn't tell him everything, but I told him enough that we could start out on a good note. I told him that I didn't like the way he was handling his new-found belief. I didn't like the way that he looked down upon every Christian because they didn't know what he knew. I told him we were in their shoes before, and a lot of them didn't know any different because they were never taught. He agreed with me that we used to be like that, but he said he never told people about what he was learning if they didn't ask. He said people always asked about what he was learning, and then he would tell them. I used to think he just wanted to tell everyone how wrong they were, but he wasn't. Most of the time, people asked him what he was studying and then they would get offended when he would tell them. Things started to heal in March of that school year. I was definitely more patient with him and more understanding of his viewpoints in the coming months. And part of me actually wanted to learn more, go figure.

That spring I took up a new sport: track. Since I had never run track, I thought that I would either do the 200- or the 400-meter races. Everyone I talked to thought I'd be a good 400-meter man. Everyone also told me it would be the hardest race. I wanted to do track to prove to myself that I didn't stop playing basketball at Southshore simply because the workouts were tough. I wanted to prove to myself that I could excel in a varsity sport at a public school; but most of all, I wanted a letterman jacket.

As the season started, the first few days of practice I was sore. I would come to find what we did on the first day of practice was not going to be nearly as hard as some of the other things we would do. I liked my track coach, and I liked that when we were done with workouts, we were done for the day. There wasn't a need to stay and run just to stay and run. And we would have meets either on Wednesdays, Fridays, or Saturdays. The day before the meet would always be light in preparation, so we weren't running hard every single day.

The first time I ran the 400 in practice was unforgettable. One would think that the athleticism in the blood of the son of a professional football player would kick in running a 400-meter race. When the race started it was two other guys and me. I was running hard but didn't realize how hard that last 100 meters was going to be. This was a race in which one basically had to sprint, and one wanted to be able to sprint the hardest down the last 100 meters to finish strong. Sprinting down the final stretch, I could feel the fatigue in my muscles. My brain was telling me one thing, while my pride was telling me another. My brain said, "Stop!" and my pride said, "You can do this." I kept going, but not without a "mug" on my face. Track people call this the look on a runner's face that shows he is clearly working hard to finish what he started. Everyone who saw me coming down the stretch said, "Look at his face!" I know I appeared straight-up crazy, because my body wanted me to stop so badly.

When I finally crossed the finish line and came in second out of three people, I dropped to the ground the second I crossed the line. People told me, "Jeremy, get up, man. It's worse if you lie down." I told them, "I know, man, but I gotta stay down here." I asked Coach my time, and he said, "Sixty-six seconds." Disgraceful. But taking into account this was my first time running track and the second week of practice, I had to get better.

Thankfully that was the last workout of the day. When I got ready to go to my car, my legs literally felt like Jello. I was about to fall over again. I knew I had worked them; and I was proud, but at the same time knew I wasn't fit for track yet. But I was having fun. The thing that I liked most about track was the fun with the other people. No matter how tired people were or how hot it was outside, every time we passed each other, girl or guy, everyone was always encouraging. "Keep it up. Good job, man. Keep going," the total opposite of Southshore. I knew I would finish the season, still I had to take my teammates' positive energy and turn it into a will to race.

The first meet I remember was on a cold, drizzly Saturday. The meet was a special one because many schools from around the state came to participate, and the events lasted from 8 a.m. to 6 p.m. I was running the 400 in the last race of the day. It was 5:30 and the 4X400 meter race. There was freshman Alan Ford, junior Mark Hudson, another person, and me. Add to the setting that it had been drizzling all day but had never once really start raining.

My dad was at that meet and he was excited to see his son run arguably the toughest race in the world; definitely one of the toughest races in track. When I got up to the line, the rain started coming down harder. The gun fired and I took off. No sooner than the gun fired did it start to really come down. Running made it seem like it was coming down harder. Instead of being in the back of the pack, I was leading the rear to a spread-out pack, and I wasn't as far behind as I thought I would be. As I was creeping around the second turn into the last 100 meters I kicked it up a notch. I tried to remember what I was taught: stay light on my feet, stay on the balls of my feet, don't clench my fists, dig deep, run. As I was doing all of these things I was gaining on the second-place runner from Independence. I was literally neck and neck with him for about a good 30 meters. I said to myself, *I'm going to get second, I'm going to get second.* A little me inside my head was jumping ecstatically as I was almost about to pass the opposing runner by a few inches. Then my body did a reality check. It was almost like I hit a wall. My body slowed about 30 percent, in my mind I said, *I'm going to get third* *HUFF* *I'm going to get third.* It didn't bother me because I ran a great race. Our team came in last place, but I found out that I had run the 400 in 59 seconds! That was my best time of the whole year. I was tired, wet, and hurting, and I had just run my best time. I was happy. When I got into the stands Dad said, "That monkey jumped on your back, didn't he?" Then he changed his mind and said, "It was more like a bear actually." It felt, and I'm sure looked like, something literally jumped on my back to slow me down because I slowed so abruptly near the end of the race. I just laughed because I knew it was true.

When my dad, mom and I got home, we watched the video my mom had taken of my race. I looked like I hit a stone wall. My dad was narrating the movie, "OK, the monkey was running around the track, and it jumped on his back (pointing to my teammates behind me), then it got him, and then…wait for it…right there, bam, it jumped on your back!" It was a funny sight to see. I raced hard and don't regret not getting second because I know I was pushing my body hard and wasn't holding anything back. My cousin Shari had a different opinion. She said, "Jeremy, why do I keep hearing about you *not* getting second place! I hate hearing, 'Jeremy *almost* got second!'" I told her I tried; she told me to try harder. That was easy for her to say; she stopped running track after the first 400 she attempted. During practice she walked the last 50 meters. I couldn't believe she gave up; but she said, "Ain't no way. I'm done."

One practice we had a guy come in who helped coach football. He just came in for the day, thankfully, because he worked our 400 group so hard that day. We had already run four 200 meters for our coach at three-fourths speed before this guy came in. He had us sprint a half-mile, then jog one. Then we had to sprint a 400-meter, then jog it. Then we had to rotate sprinting and walking five 200 meters. At last, we had to sprint a 100. After practice was over he told me, "Thank you, son. Good job." I told him, "Thank you, Coach." I remember this as if it were yesterday. I got my bag, walked to my car, which seemed on the other end of the school parking lot, and just sat in my jeep with my door opened. I just sat and sat and sat. I was so tired. I was happy to have done the whole practice to the best of my ability and finish it. When I left to go home I was pretty proud of myself.

I would go on to have good races and bad races. One of my coaches even put me on shot-put. That was horrendous. He didn't do it again. But the conference was the biggest race of my season. I didn't work as hard as I did that season to not run in the biggest race of the year; and because I wasn't going to state, conference was the big one for me. When I asked Coach if I were going to race in conference, he told me it would depend on how I did that day. In my mind I had to race strong.

The gun fired; I started to sprint. Everyone was ahead of me, but I was running a good race for myself. When I got on the last hundred meters I knew I had to kick it into overdrive if I were to have any chance of racing in conference. As I started to go into overdrive, I heard my mom yelling, "Go boy! Go!" I was running so hard I started to inch on the heels of one of my fellow teammates. All I heard my teammates in the stands saying was, "He's passing him! He's passing him!" My mom and teammates were my remaining fuel to pull up behind this guy and overtake him. I beat him with a time of 58.4 seconds. Nothing spectacular, but for coming from the beginning of the season with 66 seconds, I was extremely proud.

The rest of the week, getting ready for conference, I could tell that the guy I beat held a little resentment toward me. It wasn't anything serious, but I could tell. As conference time came, I talked to my teammate Alan Ford, saying we were going to run the 400 in 36 seconds and a lot of other nonsense (36 seconds has *never* and probably will never be accomplished) about how we were going to eat an entire pizza all by ourselves since after this race, track season was over for us. I ran 58 seconds again, but we didn't win the race because our first leg started off too slow. But after the race Alan and I took a victory lap anyway. I did get my letter jacket, and proudly hung it in my room. I proved to myself that the people at Southshore drove me to stop playing basketball; I didn't quit. And for that, I could rest easy.

Sometimes I would go home and try to tell Dad about my feelings. I would try to tell him I realized I was solid after that track practice, but I couldn't find the words all the time. Mostly, I would go to him with nonsense, blathering on about snow make-up days or excessive homework. My dad would listen without really listening, because half the time I'd be talking nonsense anyway. He would say, "Really? Oh, OK." And that would be it, unless I was trying to talk to him while he was watching television. That inspired Dad's act of falling asleep on me. He would start snoring and say, "Jeremy, can you go take a nap or something?" This always amused me because I kenw he was half serious, even though he loved me and was glad I was talking to him. He had been doing that since I was able to talk. He just didn't know his son could talk so much.

That spring another chapter began. When I came home from school, I noticed something was missing from the mantle. *No way. He wouldn't.* The Sam Philipe gold, silver, and bronze Biblical figurines were gone. The Ark of the Covenant, Moses and the Ten

Commandments, Dad loved these prizes from Israel. I didn't even have to look. I knew the others weren't where they had been that morning either. During the course of the morning, or late the night before while he was studying, Dad came to believe that they were carved idols. Now they were contraband. I couldn't take him throwing them all away, and after he discarded them, I snuck into the garbage and rescued Daniel and the Lions and Sampson. I hid them in my loft for sake keeping.

A few weeks later, I heard Dad calling for me. His tone was less than Son-let's-have-a-father-son-talk. Sure enough, he was in my loft, and in his hands, the figurines that he thought he threw out. He was growling, "I-thought-I-threw-these-out! You-have-no-right-to-go-behind-me-and-disrespect-me." But the next words I made out clearly. "You are going to throw these out yourself."

How could I? He was throwing away $75,000. He could realize next week that he overdid it, and by then, the Archangel would be under tons of diapers, newspapers, and sludge. I had disregarded Dad's wishes to save his precious art in the first place. To throw them out now, well, it defeated the reason I hid them to begin with. But as with every other edict Reggie White gave, I found myself standing over the garbage can with Sampson in hand. I envisioned him to have looked upon Delilah in the same way. I threw the figurines so hard the sound reverberated in my ears. If somehow I threw them hard enough, Dad would snap out of it.

Later, when Aunt Maria found out that Dad threw out those figurines, she said, "Why didn't you tell me? I didn't idolize them." Maybe Dad did feel he liked them too much. I just didn't want him to regret his hasty judgment. If anyone had been sifting through our garbage during this time, they could have made a killing.

In 1991, in Tennessee, Mom and Dad had a beautiful glass etching made of The Last Supper. It hung in the opening between the dining room and the great room in our Cornelius house. Hung. Until one day while going for a Coke in the refrigerator, Dad realized that Jesus had a sunburst over his head. I knew the etching's days were numbered, but I didn't help Dad along. No sun god worship in the White house. Sure enough, Dad had me to help load it up, to drive this $10,000 representation to the dump personally (I guess to be certain of its fate), and to dispose of it. Almost in protest, the etching stood on its edge before it finally toppled over and shattered...and my hope of regaining my dad with it.

Dad did think of the etching as an image of God, and he didn't believe in having any images of God. He already made this very clear when he threw out the Jesus statues and images in our house. The other reason for our latest trip to the dump was the Messiah's halo around his head, a "burst of light." He had learned from Michael Rood, a teacher of the Old Testament and roots of the Bible, that the "burst of light" behind Jesus' head is actually a sunburst, a representation of the sun god Ra. He also taught that most of the old statues and pictures of Mary and the baby Jesus were really statues and pictures of the sun god and his mother. I never realized it until he mentioned it, but it made perfect sense. Again, as for the Last Supper, he wouldn't sell it either, nor any of the other things he said had to go. No devil in our house, no devil in anyone else's.

There was always this unspoken battle between my father and me, because I would talk about it with my mom and sister, and he probably knew I was. It made him feel all that more alone, and he probably started asking how to get closer to me. The only way he knew how to insert himself into anything was to present his new findings in the Bible to us. He was not there a lot when he was play-ing football, because he was playing, preaching, working on a busi-ness deal, working out, or sleeping. I wanted to be mad at him, but I couldn't, because he never had a real father or father figure to look to as a role model. I wanted to be able to yell at him and make him feel lower than dirt for every direction he was taking me. I wanted to be able to scream and tell him he was doing all these good things for so many people, but he didn't even know how to open up to his own children. I wanted to curse him out, and I had never even said any of those words before even with my friends. All of these things I wanted to do, but I couldn't. Something was holding me back. That something was God.

Later that week I apologized to him for what I had done. He accepted it, and we sat down and talked man to man about why I thought he didn't make any sense. I told him that almost anything could be construed an image; but I think God meant making a literal idol, one that people know as an idol, similar to the golden calf in the book of Exodus. Those people made that cow purposely to worship it. I told him that if the law were not to make a graven image of anything, then we would practically have to be blind to not consider anything an idol. Finally, he agreed with me. At least we understood each other. For now, there was a Band-Aid on our problem with the graven image issue.

In school I was showing signs of stress without knowing it. Another teacher I liked was Mrs. Amy Hallman, my creative writing teacher. Every day we did fun little writings; and each week, we would bring in a book and read for the entire class period to sample good, and sometimes bad, writing. During this volcanic period at home, Mrs. Hallman was the only teacher who acknowledged she felt like something wasn't right with me. To know a student that well was kind of shocking to me. In the beginning of the year, I always participated in class and always wrote things with enthusiasm; but later in the term one day she wrote on my paper, "Jeremy, is everything OK? You seem to have been zoning out lately." I thought to myself, *If you only knew, and you don't want to know.* How could I tell her that I was making daily trips to the dump with our once-treasured pieces?

On top of that, Mrs. Hallman was a caring person, and she wanted all of us, who were truly interested in it, to succeed in writing. She made me submit my poetry to the national *Celebration of Young Poets* contest; and it actually got published in the spring of 2003 in a book for middle school and high school poetry. That was a pretty proud moment to look at my poetry in a nationally published book. Getting my poetry published reassured me that I had a natural gift. I did not intend to waste it.

Since my dad continued Bible studies with us on Saturdays, we ultimately stopped going to church on Sundays. My dad's understanding of the Bible stated the Sabbath was on Saturday, therefore we should have church on Saturday. The reasoning wasn't just that Sunday was named after a pagan god, because, in fact, all the days of the week are named for other gods. Ultimately, we realized that Dad's studies were more honest and truth-seeking than any Sunday sermon we could locate. He was furious to discover what the church knew and purposefully kept quiet. He understood that all the days of the week are based on pagan gods. But Sunday and Monday as sun and moon gods, Tiu (Tuesday), Woden (Wednesday), and Fria (Friday) as Anglo-Saxon gods, and Thor (Thursday) and Saturn (Saturday) would be unexpected, and unwelcome guests in a Sunday sermon. Solstice and Christianity were not to be interconnected. We required the entire truth, not the safe truth.

I got out of the habit of going every Sunday, but also, I feel church has nothing to offer me anymore. My father took me so far in learning the Bible, the history of the Bible, Hebraic idioms, metaphors, and root words, that I do not feel that church can extend those lessons. I don't think church is bad at all. I believe in the Bible, not a particular religious view. I believe in the Old Testament and the New. I believe one has to read the Bible front to back, not back to front; and it is a handbook on how to live. The Bible interprets itself. The verses are not to be read singularly, but as a whole; and they cannot be taken out of context. I recognize the Sabbath is Saturday not Sunday, but everyone else can choose to worship the Father any day of the week in the manner of a church service. I don't feel I'm better than anyone else. And I don't think that I know everything about the Bible; but most of the churches I have attended all deal with what I like to call the "surface" issues: Jesus loves you, follow Jesus, tithe, love one another, and be patient. Rarely have I been to church where they talk about the tough things like the roots of Christmas, if we should celebrate it and/or how; or the biblical representation of Satan. No church I've attended tackles what Isaiah, Jeremiah, Obadiah, Amos and the other prophets were really advocating. The churches I've attended choose to deliver a feel-good message to start out the week, rather than give an inspirational teaching.

But like I said, that's my experience; and if church has significance in someone else's life, they should keep going. I know my reasons for nonattendance, and it largely has to do with me having teeth. I want to eat meat, not to be fed milk anymore. My dad first provided the meat. It's tough to find another chef who serves everything that I currently know about the Bible. Will I go to church when I have kids? I will absolutely go to church, because they need a foundation. The church is a great place, in my opinion, to learn the basics: why to believe in God and to be a Believer in the Lord, Father of Abraham, Isaac, and Jacob.

It doesn't deliver the "did you know" in-your-face type sermons that are clearly in the Bible and in the history of the language. A strong example of this in-depth teaching is this: read closely the chapter in Genesis in which Eve eats the forbidden fruit and God exiles Adam and Eve. One realizes that because of Adam, sin entered the world. But haven't we always been taught as believers that Eve was responsible for the downfall of man? If Eve hadn't eaten the fruit there would be no sin? It's Eve's fault, right? Hasn't that been our teaching? My dad pointed out to me that in the verse after Eve ate of the forbidden fruit, nothing happened. It was only after Adam took and ate that *then* "their eyes were opened." This is not to say that Adam is the only one responsible, but it does say that Adam finished the deed of bringing sin into the world. What would have happened if Adam had said no? Eve's eyes were not opened yet. When she was created, he had told Eve, "You are bone of my bone and flesh of my flesh." They were one in spirit, and if one of them sinned that wouldn't have ruined the human race. They were one together they needed to both sin for it to have an everlasting effect. This realization isn't hard to wrap your head around, but this is no standard, feel-good lesson.

As time went on, I would start to get psyched for prom. However, I didn't have a date. At the time I liked this one girl. Let's call her Susie. Susie and I had been hanging out a little bit, and I always talked to her in school because I liked her. When the time came I didn't know how to approach her to ask her to prom. I was shy but I knew it was up to me to ask. Normally, I am not a shy person, except when it comes to girls I like and telling them. I couldn't just go up to a girl and say, "Hey, you look good. You want to go to the movies with me or something?" I wanted to be able to be friends with someone for a while and to have a mutual understanding of whether we both liked each other. I would continue to try this dating approach in college too.

I decided to write her a poem:

Ok now it's time to make my move—
Don't panic, don't punk out; be cool.
"I know we've known each other for only so long
But, like with certain girls, I think of this song."
You're just too good to be true.
I know it may not sound new but let me express how I feel about you:
you're smart, not dumb, like some—
You're nice, caring, and don't forget silly,
And since you lived down south, you get chill….real easy.
You believe partly the same as I do in faith,
More than you know…and that's great.
Every time I question, "Do I want to be with her?"
Guess what, when I see your beauty there's the answer.
Ever since I saw you I've thought you looked good,
But I didn't know that I ever would
Be able to meet you, because I didn't know your name.
But peeps around me put you at a fame.
You stand out from the crowd just by how you look;
It's not a bad thing, it's something that sticks
In my mind for a while.
Then when you've faded out of memory, I return
to school to see your smile.
I really don't know if you think the same of me,
But unanswered questions come to be
A jumble of "what ifs."
If I let it, it will take me in a drift,

One of those dazes where your heart jumps and you feel relaxed
Because even if the day feels jacked,
Seeing and speaking with you can make the pain go away.
It didn't take a lot to write this because as you know, when
You are familiar with something it just flows like a mist.
Forgive me for being mad; I was mostly sad
Because you had a boyfriend, and he obviously made you glad;
But the way I feel just can't stay stuck
Inside me, I have to do it;
I have to be strong.
So to end it out there is a question:
With me, will you go to the prom?

I was not in love with this girl, but I did like her. All I knew was to try to coax her to go to prom with me; it's who I am. I'm a romantic.

After I gave her the poem, I was shot down. She said it was sweet, but she didn't want to go to prom this year; she was waiting for her senior year. She also said she had turned other guys down, so she didn't want it to look bad if she went with me. I remember getting a line up at the barbershop, telling the barber my woes. He said, "Man, what does turning down other people have to do with you?" I exclaimed, "That's what I said, man! I don't know; it's whatever." Later, she would find out I had liked her, and she told me I was like her brother. Isn't that always the way?

This is not the first time this had happened. I had told a girl I liked while at Southshore; a cool girl, and I still keep in touch with her today. She was flattered, but she said I was like her brother. My mom's opinion is that these girls that said I was too brotherly were probably too fast for me to begin with. The word was out that I didn't kiss on the mouth, much less anything else physical. While they respected the ideal, they weren't ready to commit to it themselves. "Jeremy's a husband, Mrs. White; and these girls want a boyfriend," Cherie told my mom at a basketball game.

Everyone at Hopewell knew that I was saving myself for the woman I would marry. The reason I didn't get picked on is the way I carried myself; I commanded respect. I didn't go around flaunting that my dad was a football player or that we had lots of money. I didn't go out and buy a Porsche because, in fact, I loved my Jeep. I didn't go around telling people, "Hey, do you know who I am?" Because of my humility people respected me and each decision I made. If I had gone around school with an enormous ego and still had been a virgin, I'm sure I would have been a target. The guys would have said, "Yeah, you're Reggie White's son, but you still ain't got none." But not wanting to flaunt my identity made them see my character. And they respected my decision to wait.

There was nothing I could do about not having a date just then. My mom told me that Brittany Robinson, one of our family friends, wanted to go with me. My dad had played football with her father, Eugene Robinson in Green Bay. We saw them on and off because he lived on the other side of town. I called and asked her, and she said yes. I was excited not to ask a complete stranger, and I had known her since we were little.

Finally the day came, my first prom. Taylor and his date and Brittany and I all went to the prom in a limo. I was going to drive my dad's Mercedes, but the people all backed out who were supposed to go with Taylor in the already rented limo; so I decided, after much coaxing from our families, to go with him. We had fun, though. Unfortunately, Brittany didn't know anyone. Basically I had to dance only with her. I liked her, but I wanted to dance crazy with my friends. I had a pretty good time though. When we got back that night I was tired and ready to go home. So was Taylor's date. Brittany and Taylor however were too crunk; they were ready to party. At Taylor's house, sipping some sparkling grape juice, just chillin', we laughed about people's bizarre behavior at the prom. Then I took Brittany back to my house, and she stayed the night (far, far away from me, for all the critics out there).

Later, I would go on to finish my junior year with perfect attendance and a 4.0 average. I signed up for *The Siren,* Hopewell's award-winning newspaper because Mrs. Hallman, the adviser, suggested I interview with the staff. She wanted me to put my skills to practical use as an entertainment writer. Video game reviews, of course.

That summer I worked at a sub restaurant, and my crush on Alyce deepened. So deep, in fact, that when I thought about my commitment not to kiss until the altar, I realized that I probably wouldn't make it. Not just because of Alyce, but because the idea of affection, of love, showed me I would kiss a girl before I got married. I would later tell her in a poem that I liked her, but she didn't respond to me for about three weeks (This poem thing wasn't working for me). She managed to avoid me in high school halls. I took that as, "Look, if I talk to you I might ruin a friendship we have, I'd rather not mention it and let our friendship keep going. I hope you understand." I'm sure that's the soft version, but I feel better about that one. I never heard those words from her, but it was a good move. We were better off friends.

11

The first day of being a senior in high school was not all it was hyped up to be. I was a little disappointed there was no '04-'05 rivalry like the previous year; '05 hardly put up a fight.

Within the first few days, I decided to be more involved in school and to strengthen my college résumé. I became the women's varsity basketball manager. And I deserved every bit of the credit on my college application. I knew a few of the girls on the team, most importantly, my sister. Since Jecolia was on the squad, I helped my parents taking her to and from practice. I went to all the games, I washed all their clothes, I even helped out in their drills. It was fun; I was part of the team. I earned my keep, and I lettered. They started to become my family. And even though we all were not really close, it was as if I had a bunch of sisters. We joked around and were supportive of one another. And I knew the dirt: who didn't like whom and vice versa. I was needed.

Our women's basketball team had a good year. We finished above .500, and had a pretty decent shot at moving on in the first round of the playoffs. That game was a heartbreaker. The girls didn't play poorly, but the other girls played extremely well. The other team wasn't missing any shots. Any. After the game the opposing coach said he had never seen his girls hit that number of shots in any game before. They had hit 80 percent of their shots. Any basketball team, male or female, hitting 80 percent is going to be winning games. A lot. Since it was either win or go home, it was the last game of the season for us.

That year I was consumed with the school newspaper since it was an actual class. The first few days of class we brainstormed types of articles to be written. I gravitated toward entertainment. I mentioned that there should be a review of new video games. The adviser thought that was a great idea. Since I wanted (and still would like to) write for a video game magazine after college, I thought that it would be good practice to write video game reviews for *The Siren.*

The trouble I found was writing for an audience who already understood video games. One of the chief editors said she couldn't understand my article. I disagreed with her, so I only changed one very minute thing; and Mrs. Hallman, my former creative writing teacher and the adviser, said it was a great article. She was famous for being tough on articles, so I knew it was good. I learned a lot that year about writing, but the article I am proudest of is the human interest piece I did on Taylor Johnson, our family friend.

Taylor has an extraordinary gift for music. This man can make beats off the top of his head, he can compose the greatest of ballads on the piano, and he can virtually hear any song and play it by ear within 20 minutes. Did I mention he can't read a note of music? Along with putting together his own music, sometimes, as something on the side, he would write lyrics to be rapped or sung. His gifts are amazing.

Because he is my friend, and many at school weren't aware of his talent, I decided to write the article about him. I interviewed him and went to his house to photograph him by his piano. When I got there he said, "Hold on one second!" He ran upstairs to put on a suit to look professional. I still laugh at the photograph because he didn't bother to put on any shoes. The camera didn't capture his sock feet, but I knew. The 19-year-old boy jumped into a suit, slid in white socks to the piano, and sat down as if he were Mozart. Craziness. I wrote one of the best articles, I think, that I had ever written. Every quote was in the right place and style, every description was in the perfect spot and every word flowed into the next. When she graded my article, Mrs. Hallman highlighted it in the staff meeting, saying, "This is excellent!" I knew I had nailed it.

The Siren wasn't free to publish, and it wasn't cheap to create either. But because we didn't charge students for newspapers, we had to make money through advertisements and donations. In class one day, I suggested we have a male auction, and at the end of the auction, we could have a little dinner on stage for all the people who won and participated. After a little tweaking, and a giant debate on what to name the event, everyone loved this idea. It took a little doing, but we finally worked it out. The principal wanted us to open it up to boys and girls, but Mrs. Hallman didn't think it was a good idea to auction off girls.

We had 20 guys volunteer to be auctioned. After choreography, catering, and practice, our highest bachelor went for $57, and our cheapest dinner date went for six bucks. When it came time for me to go on, I was in a sharp red suit with a candy-cane cane (since it was around Christmas time). My friend, Cherie was bidding on me. People bid faster than I thought, and before I knew it I was up to $22. At least I got away from the single digits. Later, Cherie told me that someone else was trying to win me, and she kept looking at her as if to say, "Girl, if you don't stop bidding I'm not going to have enough money to be able to get J." After the auction, the dinner on the stage was fun. When the music came on Cherie and I started doing the Love Slide. "Scholars for Dollars" was a success, and we raised over $800 for the newspaper. Mrs. Hallman was impressed.

Later I went on my first spring break trip without parents, family, or siblings, to Myrtle Beach, South Carolina. During that time, Mom and Jecolia went to New York; and my dad called a Hebrew Scholar, Nehemia Gordon, to teach him more Hebrew and the Bible. Before I left he said, "Jeremy, we are gonna have so much fun. Are you sure you don't want to stay?" I probably rolled my eyes when I said I was sure I was still going. I kind of felt bad leaving him there since my mom and sister were gone. But I was trying to do my own thing for once by myself, and he had Nehemia anyway. Though I was psyched to go solo to Myrtle Beach with my friends, I thought that I would have a better time than I did. We went to a dance club where one had to be 18 to enter. I was two months away from being 18, but they let me in twice. Sometimes freedom isn't all that.

Although I didn't want to submerge myself in our beliefs like Dad, he persisted. Again, he did not move away from our core belief in God and that he came to the earth in the form of man. But while the specifics of what we believed were changing, the base of what we believed was still strong. I didn't want to learn anything new because I was only 17, and I already knew more than my peers. I wanted to be normal. I wanted to be able to feel that if I was going to church and hearing the sermon that I was doing fine. But learning from Dad, I found out that little things I had been doing for years were wrong. Certain things I was eating were bad for me. Holidays I was celebrating had nothing to do with Christ at all. The English word hell in the Bible should never have been translated that way, because it means "grave" in Hebrew. I found out all these things before I was 17. I could have debated a Christian theologian on why Acts 10 was specifically about Peter's prejudice against Gentiles and not about God calling all foods clean. At 17, I knew *gentile* means *pagan*, but had been accepted into English translation as "a person who is not a Jew." I could have done this when I was 16, and I hadn't even been to seminary. Every time Dad learned something, he rushed me like I was on the other side of the line from him. And I felt like he was pounding his knowledge into me.

When *Angels and Demons* and *The Da Vinci Code* were released, my parents immediately read them. My dad told me many times to read these two books, that much of the stuff he was finding out about Christianity (the worship of the Sun god, for example) was there; and that while there was national attention from churches trying to discredit Dan Brown, Dad knew they were true. He was so happy to find other people who were knowledgeable about this information. Dad was finding that Christians, pastors, preachers, and "men of God" knew of what he was speaking, but they didn't care and did not want to share it. They were specifically and admittedly worried that they would lose their congregation by recognizing such facts, and they would lose their income. For my dad to find a nationally published bestseller to include the very things he was learning directly was overwhelming and exciting. I didn't want any part of it, so I didn't read them. Later, though, this would change.

When my dad would stress me out I needed to get away to the movies. Before I could drive, my mom would drop me off. Even if I went alone, the movie theater was one place I could escape from the world. I still do it today. I'll go to anything from G to R movies, as long as it entertains me, and I can break loose from the routine of my life. My dad was no different. I would grow up to learn that he went to the movies a lot to get away too. My mom would ask him, "Hey Reggie, you wanna go see this movie?" He would say he already saw it. Then she would say, "Why didn't you ask me to go?" He would say he just wanted to see it. It's not that we didn't like going with people, but when the time and need came, we both would escape, regardless of company. In a dark theater, no one would ask for an autograph. It was his sanctuary. And without realizing it, we shared it.

One day Dad called from his room, "Jeremy, come here." Even though I knew I couldn't have done anything wrong, naturally, I thought, *What could I have possibly done?* He pointed to the television and said, "Look at this." An old video clip of the Packers playing the Vikings in the mid-'90s showed the ball snapped and former Eagles wide receiver Cris Carter had to block my dad so Dad wouldn't sack Warren Moon. Cris had hesitated for a second and my dad noticed Cris was the only one apparently blocking him. He grabbed Cris from underneath his arms and threw him to his left about ten feet. Cris flew through the air like a leaf and landed, tumbling on his side. By the time Cris stood and shook off the thrashing, Dad had already sacked Warren Moon. I thought that was the funniest mismatch on the line. Dad couldn't stop laughing.

"Jeremy," he said, "during this same game I tossed the offensive lineman on the first play, number 76, I mean manhandled him, on the very first play of the game. The next time we lined up he said, 'Oh shit. This is gonna be a long day.'" This story was doubly funny to me because not only had I heard my dad curse (even if only in repeating someone), but I realized if only there were a way to really hear what is said between players at the line, the game could be so much more entertaining. Certainly there would be more stories to tell on ESPN.

As my senior year slipped away, I became a little stressed about where to go to college. I knew I wanted to be a journalist and write for a video game magazine, so I knew I needed to go to a school that had a great communications program. The only school that was standing out at the time was the University of North Carolina at Chapel Hill.

My visit there was a good one because we didn't have a tour guide. My neighbor was a junior at Chapel Hill, and she showed my mom and me around campus. I went to the bookstore, I got to see her dorm, and we walked to many different places in the immediate area. It seemed like a nice school, but for some reason the word "Chapel" made it sound boring. I knew I shouldn't base my decision on that, but I do remember thinking it. I sent in my UNC application. Out of nowhere my mom told me, "Aunt Maria's friend's daughter goes to a school called Elon University near Greensboro. She told me they have a great communications program. Do you want to go visit?" I gave in. When I found out it was a private school, however, I was not too enthusiastic, because I had been in private schools all my life. Later, I realized that there are almost 5,000 students at Elon, and I wouldn't feel like I was in a "private" school. Another reason I wasn't too enthusiastic was I thought that the people there would be snotty. And ultimately, they would think I was snotty. It would cost a pretty penny to attend Elon, but as far as private schools go, it is a good deal, especially for out-of-state students who have the same tuition.

When my aunt, my mom, and I went to visit Elon, it was a dreary day. I didn't have a good first experience; and after I left, I didn't really want to go to Elon. We stopped by Winston-Salem State, a historically Black College that is 70 percent female. When we arrived on campus and saw a girl who had gone to my high school, she told us about the school. My aunt said, "Do you guys drink here?" Calmly, the girl said, "This is a dry campus." My aunt said, "Sure it is." Aunt Maria wasn't being sarcastic, but she was eager for me to go to Elon and only Elon. She found something negative to say about any other school, especially Winston-Salem State. "It's too close to the highway." "You don't need to be looking at all these girls or their butts for that matter." "It doesn't seem organized." She was just saying everything she could think of to keep me from the school. What she didn't realize was her badmouthing every other school discredited Elon to me. I applied anyway. So far I had only applied to two schools and didn't know if I would like either one of them.

In November 2003, my dad had a Barbrit for me and a Barbrat for my sister. These traditions are similar to a Bar Mitzvah and a Bat Mitzvah, except we aren't Jewish. Dad said this was what they did in Biblical times. He explained with authority that this was what the Bible instructs us to do with our children when we deem them a man or a woman. He invited nearly everyone we knew to celebrate. Behind tears he said, "Because all of our kids leave us one day; and honestly, I'm not ready for that." He choked up for a second and quickly regained his composure. My sister and I completed our readings partly in Hebrew and partly in English; but ironically, and neither of our parents knew this, I read my sister's reading and she read mine, a simple mistake.

After they each gave us a blessing, and had a trusted family friend bless us as well, Dad presented my sister and me each a ring. The rings read in Hebrew "Kadosh," meaning *holy*, which literally means *set apart*. These were our promise rings. We are to wear these rings until we get married and replace them with our wedding rings, letting our spouses know, "I saved myself for you." It was a great moment, and those rings were shining. Then my mom made a surprise announcement. From a piece of paper she read, "Dear Jeremy, After looking over your application for entry into Elon University, it is my pleasure to tell you that you have been accepted for the Fall 2004 term." I was proud, but I was not as happy as one would think, because I still wasn't sure if I was going there or not. At least I had something to fall back on. We had a celebration, and my cousin Shari's dad was the DJ. That was when I first saw a set of turntables and scratched a record. Unbelievable.

Still, Dad and Mr. Keith took Taylor and me to visit the University of North Carolina at Greensboro and the North Carolina A&T. On the way, we were listening to Taylor's beats, and since our dads were very much into the Hebrew language, they liked a track that had a Middle Eastern tune to it. They were both acting like big kids that day.

Because UNCG did not have a journalism program, I did not want to go there. I didn't like North Carolina A&T too much, either, and neither did my dad, Mr. Keith, or Taylor. We all got the same impression with the vibe from the people and the place as a whole that it was too much like high school. Elon or Chapel Hill were still my top choices.

In February, Elon invited minorities one weekend to stay with current students on campus to encourage their acceptance. Before going, I asked God to let me have peace about where He wanted me to go. If it was Elon I wanted to feel it in my spirit. I stayed with a student named James Brewer, who at the time was on line to be part of the fraternity Phi Beta Sigma. He was already busy as it was, but he was also a music major. He was a nice guy to talk to and to ask questions. I got dropped off with three black girls. Since I was a prospective student, I was like a pet. They called me their "pet negro."

I spent the day with them and met some of their friends. They showed me around campus. I asked them a lot of questions because I wanted to get a clear idea what I would be getting into if I attended Elon that fall. That night I had so much fun at a party. The DJ was good, the dancing was fun, and for the first time I saw a party hop, black sororities and fraternities dancing in rhythm and in a circle. A line of people dance repeatedly over and over to create a party hop. It reminded me of the dancing that I did at the Feast of Tabernacles in tenth grade. It was fun to see the similarities between Greek life and Hebrew life. And that night I would learn about the "late-night meal run," a staple of college life. The next morning my mom came, and we went to a talk about the school. Before we left we took a picture with Maya, April, and Whitney. My mom always takes pictures. Maya and Whitney came out in their pajama pants, because on a Saturday morning at a college campus, everyone is either asleep or passed out from the night before. When Myaa heard my mom tell her to get out of bed and take a picture, she was shocked and kind of amused.

On the way home, I felt such a peace about Elon. I enjoyed the people there; and I realized that even if some of the people were snotty, there were still 4,500 other people to choose from as friends. I knew that's where I was going. I told my mom that even if Chapel Hill accepted me (and they hadn't responded yet) I was not going. I was going to Elon in the fall.

In the same month there was the National Honor Society induction. I was nominated and accepted. I was number 44 out of 350 people in my class, and I displayed great leadership outside the classroom.

The keynote speaker for the induction was none other than my dad. Usually when he came to speak at my school I was embarrassed. My dad was the greatest defensive end, arguably defensive player, to ever play the game of football. He was a loving father and a loving husband, and he did everything in his power to serve God. Why would I be embarrassed? Everywhere I went my father was the one speaking. He spoke at home, he spoke at church, he spoke at other people's churches, he spoke so much that he got paid to speak. Every school I'd ever been to invited him to speak. I heard the same speech from the same person, and I couldn't get as excited as some of my peers because he was my father; to me he wasn't Reggie White.

But there was something different about that night. Since I had talked with my dad and told him what frustrated me with him, our relationship started to heal. The alienation and annoyances causing me to one-day-yell-at-him-when-I-was-eighteen-and-never-talk-to-him-again, were draining out. I felt at peace. Finally, I was proud to see my dad up there in a position of honor, and I didn't care who knew that he was my dad. I was getting closer and closer to my father after holding such resentment against him for taking away my normalcy in all senses of the word. For the first time, when I looked at a family picture I wanted to cry. I wanted to cry for all the things I thought badly about him. I wanted to cry for all the things I wanted to say to him out of spite. I wanted to cry for all the things I wanted to do to rebel against him when he was simply trying to help me be a more Godly man, a man's man, an honorable and respected man. My father had the best intentions for me, and for a while I wanted to spit it in his face and tell him I didn't want anything to do with it. But most of all, I wanted to cry because I felt I truly loved my father. I loved him for his vigor, for the things I didn't like about him, and for trying to be a father when he didn't have one to model himself after. That's why I wanted to cry.

After the speech, everyone got a copy of his autobiography, *In the Trenches*, and he would later sign every one of them. I still haven't gotten mine. That was a great night because he was so proud of me. I could see it in his face and hear it in his voice. Also, he was proud of every single student in that room who worked hard to be in the National Honor Society. For me, that night wasn't about getting accepted into an organization, it was about how much I loved my dad. No longer was it just three words that little kids say to their parents; I could feel each syllable of "I love you."

About a month later, Taylor got his acceptance letter from Chapel Hill about the same time I was deterred. Sure I felt bad, but I knew I didn't want to go to Chapel Hill. Still, I wanted them to want me. I sent in my acceptance into the National Honor Society and my transcript with a 4.0+ GPA for my first semester as a senior to see if I could get accepted later.

Prom 2004 was a great time. I went to two proms. In the summer of 2003, my mom told my sister's AAU basketball team that if any of them needed a prom date, I was their man. She was joking, but one girl took her seriously. She called me out of nowhere and asked me to go to her prom. She wasn't interested in me, but she knew that I'd be fun to go with. Mom said, "I didn't think they'd take me seriously, Jeremy!" She looked very elegant that night. We had a good time.

The prom that mattered to me the most, however, was my own prom. I took a girl named Jennifer Anne Lee, whose mom swears up and down that we are going to get married (sorry, Mrs. Lee). Jennifer and I were friends, and my formal invitation was something like, "Hey Jennifer, you're going to prom with me, OK?" She said, "OK, but asking would have been better." I apologized and then asked her, and she said yes. We were so fly that night when we drove to prom in my dad's teal 1951 Mercury. We got to prom a little later than expected and only had so much time to dance because we wanted to take our pictures first before we got sweaty.

My winter league basketball team stunk badly. Instead of running track, because I was so out of shape, I decided to play recreational basketball in the spring. I prayed for a good team. My prayers were answered, and I was on a well-rounded team that played well together. We went 7-0 at the start of the season, beating our first team 88-52. Our first loss was to a team that was also good, 73-70. But losing hurt that night like we had won no previous games. One would rather lose the first game and then go on to win the next seven than to win seven then lose one.

My frustration got the best of me that night. The scorekeeper left off a point for us, and one of our best players got in a scuffle with the referee. After the game, I kicked over a chair, and the referee thought it was my teammate. Later, when I told the ref that I had done it, he didn't believe me. Our whole team just had to walk away from that one and come back the next week to take care of business.

One player dislocated his shoulder during a game, and we only had six people left to play. I took a commanding lead of the team. I didn't score the most points, but I just played a bigger leadership role than usual. Still, we lost by one point, 61-60.

Since everyone made the playoffs and we had the best record, we were scheduled to play the team we had beaten earlier in the season 88-52. Throughout the game we were not the same team we were when we had beaten them. We were getting outplayed, and one of our fastest guys fouled out. The other team took full advantage. One of their players, Chris Hall, had played for Hopewell's Varsity basketball team. He was a senior too. He had such a great game; we could not stop him. Also, I think the fact he is four inches taller than I (and I was about 6'1-6'2 at the time) might have had something to do with it. They beat us, and Chris' team would go on to win the championship. Everyone in the league knew we had the best team, but we just didn't show up that game. That's the part that hurts the most, when you play a game you know you are supposed to win and you lose it. I could relate to my dad losing to the Denver Broncos in Super Bowl XXXII; we should have and could have beaten them, but we didn't. That's the reason, Dad would later tell me, that this loss hurt so badly.

After losing the first game of the season, however, my dad had a little surprise waiting for me at home. On the cover of what looked like a car read, "Jeremy, I am so proud of you." He also had a bootleg cover on which he wrote with a Sharpie, "Elon, here we come." Since he owned part of a Chevrolet dealership, he had located a yellow SSR for me. I was so surprised. The fact that I had just lost the first game of the season didn't bother me anymore. I drove it to school the next day. I had been driving a Jeep that I had purchased with my own money. The SSR was a huge upgrade. While I didn't quite like the attention in it, I didn't want to be unappreciative. I was starting to come around, maybe I could handle a little flash.

I would have to get past some confrontations before graduation day. First would be senior skip day. I hadn't missed a day of school since tenth grade. I had perfect attendance my junior year, and I wanted to have it again my senior year. When senior skip day came around, I went to school. Later, I found out that people with perfect attendance until the week before were still going to get a perfect attendance award because the awards were already printed. As it turns out, I could have skipped that day.

However, I wasn't the only senior in school that day. One of the planners, our class president, Taylor Johnson, was also there. I said, "Taylor, why in the world are you here? Didn't you plan senior skip day?" He said, "Yeah, dude, isn't it funny? Right now Mr. York is going to different parks where seniors are supposed to be hanging out and trying to punish them for not being at school; and here I am doing nothing at school but laughing." I couldn't believe that the man who planned senior skip day came to school.

Near the end of the year I was ready to get out of school like many of my peers. High school was becoming more annoying than fun, and we were ready to move on to the next point in our lives. However, just before the end, some of the students, including Taylor and Alyce, were asked to raise money for the senior class breakfast and raffle prizes. Since it was still a new school at three years, there weren't many traditional senior privileges, but it was a work in progress. Seven people were asked to participate in raising money for the senior breakfast. The senior sponsor, Ms. Apex, spent her own money to buy scratch-off pads for each of us. The fundraiser gimmick was to have different people scratch off a piece of the card, to show a donation anywhere from $1-$5 depending on what they scratched. The point was to get all the scratches that would equal $100. If we completed one scratch card we raised $100. The instructions read that we were responsible for all the money on the cards. I interpreted that to mean if any of the cards were scratched we were responsible to have that money. I took three cards just in case I could get that many people to donate. I only completed one, and many people didn't complete any. In truth, at the end of the year, people are about donated out. And to subject nearly graduated seniors to one more project is risky.

On the day we needed to turn in our cards, Ms. Apex said we were supposed to come up with the rest of the money we didn't get. We were all stunned; we didn't think we owed money for not completing a card that wasn't even scratched. She said, "I took money out of my own pocket, having my husband ask me why I took $300 out of our account. I haven't even broke even because you guys didn't do your job."

Naturally, we were all in a fit because we didn't ask her to use her own money. Also, what I was hearing is that even though I completed one card, since I took three cards I was supposed to have another $200 from somewhere else. I didn't even scratch the other two cards; essentially, I just held them in case I did more fundraising. The explanation of our paying for the rest of the cards didn't make sense. It was a fundraiser. She was telling us that basically it was a "debt card." Whatever we didn't come up with, we were in debt to the school. She threatened to pull our diplomas if we did not come up with the money. All seven of us were stunned, and we were not going to let her get away with this.

The other senior sponsor, Coach O., said that Ms. Apex had lied to him that we knew all about what we were getting into. What's worse is she complained to my senior AP English teacher, Ms. Little, and said that we were to blame for the cancellation of the senior breakfast. I was in Ms. Little's class at the time. I wanted to leave the room because I couldn't believe how childish the supposed adults in charge at my school were acting. Interestingly, the situation vanished. No pulled diplomas. No explanation.

Finally the day came. And while I appreciated all my high school memories, I was more excited to be graduating. On commencement day I could not stop smiling. Going in, my tassel came off my hat, and I almost walked in the arena without a tassel, but I fixed it moments before. I told my mom where to sit, but because she got there a little later than expected, she was in the same section, but all the way up top. Walking in to "Pomp and Circumstance," I looked but didn't see my dad anywhere. I wondered if he would be late, if he got stuck in traffic. I knew he had missed things before, but surely he wouldn't miss this day. Just as we were all sitting down, I saw him wave at me and give me a thumbs-up. Everyone who needed to be there was there. My cousins, my aunt and uncle, my mom and dad, and my sister, who was singing in the choir that day, were all there. While I was seated, waiting for my row to stand, one boy crossed the stage, doing the A-town stomp sounding like he could have broken the stage. I told myself, "He better not break that stage; I gotta get across it and graduate." As my row rose, I said to myself, "I am graduating, yeaaahh!" As they called my name, "Jeremy Reginald White," I wooped and hollered and threw my fist up. I couldn't get the smile off my face.

One day during the summer, I was watching television in my parents' bedroom, and I heard this loud coughing noise down the hall. I thought a movie character was being stabbed in my house, trying to cough and scream, "Ahhhh!!" I called out, "What's going on?!" and started moving toward the kitchen. Through the gagging I hear, "Everything's OK! Everything's OK. I just drank this garlic too fast." My dad's face looked as if someone made him swallow his own pee. He said, "I just juiced some garlic because I heard it was good for you. And I drank some but I didn't realize how potent it was." I couldn't believe him; that was a five-year-old explanation. But I was still concerned. He added, "I'm going to just start taking the garlic pills." The garlic had burned his esophagus so much he would never do that again. I watched him wipe his teary eyes and shake his head one more time.

My dad asked me if I wanted to play Madden. I told him it wouldn't be fair because I'd beat him so badly. He retorted, "That's what you think. Let's play." Of course, I beat him badly. By the second quarter, I was the Cleveland Browns and he was the Packers, I was beating him 42-7. It wasn't that he didn't know how to play football, obviously; but the controller was too small for his fingers, and Madden is a bit complicated for a first timer. Later, Dad picked up a game for me called *NFL Street*. He felt he could handle this game. For the first few games I was beating him pretty good, but then he learned how to play. He was killing me, running the ball on me up and down the field as if I knew nothing about football. It was exciting because we actually had some good competition with one another. *NFL Street* was not as complicated as Madden because it was an arcade-type football game (it had simpler plays, 7-on-7 both sides of the ball, faster game play). We hadn't had so much fun playing video games with each other since we had played NFL Blitz on Nintendo 64 back in Green Bay. Sometimes Dad would pitch the football backward to a guy right as he was about to get tackled and he would go all the way to the end zone. I would say, "Dad, how did you do that?" And he would say, smiling, "Oh, that? Oh. That was a mistake." Then he would snicker because he had accidentally pressed a button that helped him. Good times.

Often I would play *NFL Street* online and have a great time. I love to play online and meet other people with my same interests. Online video games, by the way, are great for those of us who can't sleep. But there were times it wasn't so great. One night I was playing and another player in another state said, "Look at that play, you nigger!" I thought I'd gone a round with Mike Tyson. *What did he say?* I ran into Dad in the kitchen during a break and told him. His face contorted. "How do they know you are black to even think about calling you that in the first place?" he asked. I told him I wore a headset so I could talk to them while I was playing online. He told me, "Well look here, when you whoop up on him, and he's calling you a nigger, make sure you tell them, 'Well, who's the nigger now?'" I was surprised by his response because my dad was not in favor of calling anyone names. Now I realize he was shocked and had a natural instinct to protect his son. Someone had hurt his child. But it must be understood that a nigger, by its true definition, is "an ignorant person." If someone was calling me ignorant online and I beat them, who was ignorant now? The person on the other end was ignorant.

Until that incident I thought that racism was subsiding in our society today. Then I thought there must be countless people who are secretly racist out there. From then on, I never thought racism was dead in America. Sure, it might be better than it was 50 years ago; but hate breeds hate, and just because political correctness tells us not to be racist doesn't mean people who hate will stop hating. And they pass hate on to their children. It's sad.

One of the verses my dad was really big on when he was studying was Hosea 4:6. It states, "My people perish for lack of knowledge." There is more to the verse, explaining what God means when he says that, but the part my dad focused on was that people were hurting themselves for not being knowledgeable about the Bible and about God's commandments. My dad was so headstrong about learning for himself that this was the perfect verse for him to start a conversation with people to explain what he had learned. People didn't like my dad so much because he knew what he was talking about; he would say things they didn't want to hear. He was able to pull verses off the cuff and explain the Hebrew language and the traditions behind his belief. He always said that the Bible interprets itself; he knew what he was saying wasn't simply his interpretation. And I think a lot of people resented him for it.

Just before school, my dad asked me if I wanted a Cadillac Escalade EXT instead of the SSR. Originally, I had told him I wanted the Cadillac, but the SSR was not an easy car to come by so that's why he got me that, or so I thought. When I took the Cadillac, Dad said, "Thanks, son, you helped me pull one over on your mom." He hadn't been able to buy the SSR for himself, so he created a diversion, using me as an excuse to say he was buying it for me when he knew I wanted the Cadillac all along. He was very clever. He laughed about that for a while. Slick.

12

Packing for Elon University, I was excited and apprehensive. On the first day, I didn't really want everyone to see my dad; but I wasn't planning covert operations to get him into the dorm. With nearly 5,000 people at the school, I wasn't about to let it bug me if a few people knew.

While moving in, my dad went to get the key for my room, the guy who would be my Resident Advisor said, "OK, what I'm going to need for you to do is to....Hey, man! You're Reggie White! What's going on, man!!??" Cover blown. He was so excited, but I was saying to myself, "Come on, man, can't I just get my key? You're just screaming it so loud everyone's gonna hear." My dad was cool with it; he just said, "Hey, how are you?" When I got my key, I moved my stuff in. My roommate was already there; and as I went out to get more stuff, I saw my dad carrying my 20-inch TV. When I talk to people now that saw him that day, apparently they remember this big guy carrying this giant television.

While my dad and I bought my books, my mom had, according to my roommate, "organized more things in 20 minutes than I had organized in two hours." That's my mom. When my dad and I got back, my mom didn't want to leave. Dad had to tell her, "Sara, he's ready for us to go." I was hoping my mom wouldn't start crying, and she held it together. But Dad said she cried on the way home.

Letting it sink in that I was in college, I got a knock on the door. A guy working in the Elon PR department just came out with it. He blurted, "The news has been asking us to confirm if Reggie White's son goes to this school; could you either confirm or deny that you are he and that you go here." I told him, trying to hide my shock, that I'd rather him not say. He told me, "OK, I will tell them that we can neither confirm nor deny it." I couldn't believe it, and my room-mate was laughing. The next knock on the door was from two black people, telling me to be at a meeting called S.M.A.R.T. (Student Mentors Advising Rising Talent) the next day. I was curious why they didn't talk to my roommate, who was white. I explained my confusion to my roommate and then said to him, "Oh, it's because I'm black…OK, I got it now." He and I started laughing again. My mentor was a girl named Jessica Hill, who would later tell me how sexy my dad looked carrying that television, and that all she could see was this big man carrying this big TV. Sexy? How was that win-ning points?

That fall I started to DJ. Touching my uncle's records for the first time at my Barbrit started my interest; and my parents bought me turntables when they made absolutely sure I would use them. I did-n't use them much early that first semester. I met another DJ, Roddy Tate, aka DJ Kunseit (because he's the cockiest DJ on the planet), and he started to teach me a few things and helped me to develop my own style.

All throughout my first semester I would call just to talk to him. Usually when I was younger, I would call to talk to my mom and didn't care about speaking to my dad. But since we had become closer I would call and my mom would pick up the phone, and I would ask to speak to Dad. The first time I called him he was so happy to talk to me. I think he missed me a lot more than my mom did, but he just didn't want to show it. I had taken up intramural flag football when I was a freshman. At the end of the season I had one sack and two interceptions, and I pressured the quarterback a lot. I would call home and tell my dad, "Hey, Dad, I got a sack!" He said, "That's great!" While it wasn't college football, my dad knew I was having a good time. And I'm sure he liked hearing that his son, who wasn't interested in playing college or professional football, had a sack in an intramural league. He knew I was enjoying myself, and that was the most important thing to him.

I was always able to call my dad when I had a Bible question. Often my friends would ask me a question about the Bible; and I'd know what book certain verses were in, but I wouldn't know specifically where the verse or even chapter was. I could call him and say, "Hey, Dad, where does it talk about Paul saying that we shouldn't be judged by what we eat? And why wasn't he talking about the Old Testament Kosher Laws?" My dad could tell me exactly where it was and why it wasn't going against the Old Testament Law. I could always rely on him for accurate accounts. That was simply his area of expertise.

I called home one day to tell him how excited I was about my Old Testament studies class. I called home and Dad picked up. I said, "Hey, Dad, guess what?! My religion teacher was talking about Hebrew; and in the middle of the class he said, 'I don't know why people think there is a "satan," because really "satan" isn't viewed as "satan" until the New Testament. There never was a specific "satan" in the Old Testament.' Isn't that cool, Dad?! That's what you were talking about, how Satan as one being doesn't exist." He said, "Your teacher said that?" I said, "Yea, and it's just cool to know that we aren't alone in this." He said, "Yeah, that is cool." Those kinds of discussions were ones I was quickly coming to love. Talking to him about the Bible, more specifically, about things he already taught me that, at first, I didn't want to know, now became interesting to me. More and more, I was curious because I could see that we were not the only ones who believed as we did. That felt good. And being able to talk to my dad about it felt even better.

I won't lie; there were times when he'd call just to tell me something new he learned, and I didn't really want to hear it. I was busy, and I knew how my dad would get when he talked about the Bible.

The man could keep me in one spot for 20 minutes, explaining all the ins and outs of how the Hebrew word for grind means "to breed," giving a new light to the story in Judges when the Philistines captured Sampson and enslaved him to grind, or repopulate. Yes, the films show Sampson grinding grains, but Dad was always after the deeper meaning. He practically delivered a mini-sermon every time he would talk about what he had learned that day or that week. It was a blessing to have a father who still cared so much about his son's walk with God even after he was supposed to "let his son go." He still felt like it was his responsibility to at least spur me to learn the word for myself. He was pushing me toward one day learning it on my own, but he still felt a responsibility to teach me the Bible and what he was learning. I would come to value that more than I could ever know in the next few months of my freshman year in college.

In this first semester I dated a girl for three weeks. At the time I thought I was heading into a committed relationship; but of course now I know it was just "dating," not a relationship. Without going into the details of our time together, she was my first kiss. Yes, world, I didn't have my first kiss until I was 18. And while that milestone was big enough, this girl would play a much bigger role in my life.

My first kiss wasn't as much of a guilt trip as I thought it would be. I had told my parents that I wanted to wait till I got married, and I know it sounds silly, but I really wanted to. Until I was in my final months of senior year I really thought I would be able to keep that promise. In my first semester of college we were in her room watching a DVD. After the show, I decided to lean in for a kiss. I thought, *You know, I'm not going to feel guilty about this because I know even my mom had a first kiss, and she's as straight as they come.* I gave the girl a good peck on the lips. I remember thinking, *Wow, I had my first kiss,* but I didn't feel guilty. I knew that it wasn't the worst thing by a long shot. My mom would find out and wouldn't mind; my dad would never find out.

Although I wasn't sure why, I knew God had put her in my life because I felt a peace about my relationship with her, even when it was over. When I came home for fall break, I told my parents I had a girlfriend. My dad said, "You have a girlfriend!? What's her name?! When do we get to meet her!? Are you going to give her the ring (the Kadosh ring he gave me at my Barbrit)?" I had to slow him down and tell him I'd only been with her for a week. Later, I would try to see how my dad felt about this girl being white. I liked black girls and white girls, but the mixed girls appealed to me more. This girl was white, but she had smatterings of other ethnicities. She was mixed with Jewish and Greek and looked Mediterranean. Although she wasn't pale white, she was white. I wanted to know how my dad felt about that because when I was in eighth grade he told me he would rather I marry a black girl. I remembered and wanted to talk to him about it. Before I could even get a word out he told me, "Son, as long as you're happy that's all I care about." He was saying, "I trust your judgment because I raised you to be a man of God, and I know that even when you make mistakes you are still Jeremy. I trust what I've taught you." I wouldn't be able to appreciate that until a tragic day in two more months.

Alas, the girl dropped me a couple weeks after my dad said that, because she was interested in another guy. But if I hadn't dated her so quickly (which isn't in my nature) and gone home to tell him, he would have died without ever having the chance to say that to me.

I had fun the rest of the semester learning how to make good use of my time, and how to waste it. I loved the fact that I was making new friends and that they were all within walking distance. I hadn't had "neighbors" since I moved from Green Bay; and because 69 percent of the students were from out of state, and many from the regions where I had lived, I felt right at home. The girl-to-guy ratio didn't hurt either, three-to-one. Not too shabby. In December, I went home for break.

My dad was acting like a big kid. When December 19 came around, we celebrated Dad's 43rd birthday by giving him an iPod. He was so eager to use it, he kept asking me to show him how to download music. He didn't quite understand. The next morning he woke me up and said, "Jeremy, show me how to put the music on my iPod."

I was still asleep and intended to stay that way. I grumbled, "Dad, all you have to do is plug it up, and iTunes puts it on there for you. It's that simple."

"Boy, get out of bed and show me how to do this. Don't make me ask again." I couldn't believe my dad was pulling the "don't ask me twice" line when I was 18 years old. I went downstairs and showed him, and he said, "Oh that's all?"

I still couldn't focus completely. "Yes, Dad, I was trying to tell you that."

Later that night, I was watching television in the family room and Dad plopped down beside me. He said, "Jeremy, check this out." Tupac's "California Love" was blasting from the speakers he had just connected to his iPod. He liked the old school part where it said, "Shake, shake it baby, shake, shake it," because that was from an oldies song he remembered growing up. He was feeling the beat and bobbing his head. It was funny to see our relationship becoming more of a friendship, because before he didn't want us to have anything to do with secular rap. It was a transformation in our relationship that I valued dearly. I think he was finally beginning to see me as a man, not a kid. And I was seeing him as a friend, not so much as a dad. He knew what he put me through. I stuck with it, and I respected him even though I disagreed with him terribly.

My dad would sit us down and tell us about the translation of the Bible from Hebrew to English. One of his concerns was not only that a lot was lost in translation just because of the language, but that some scholars responsible for the translation changed things on purpose. There was one passage he gave us that had to do with keeping the Law of Moses. In the book of Matthew chapter 23, verse 3, it could be construed that Jesus was saying to the people to keep the Law of Moses. Another passage in Matthew sounded like Jesus was denouncing the Law of Moses given by God. It couldn't be both, and my dad wanted to find out why this was so different. When he went to Israel by himself in October of 2003, he came back with a wealth of knowledge and a book of Matthew written on one side in Hebrew and the other side in English. As he read us the passages he pointed out in the book of Matthew the translators left out the word amar from the Hebrew to the English. Jesus was not denouncing the Law of Moses in Matthew; he was denouncing the oral law, the extra laws that were made up by men such as the Sadducees and Pharisees. Just one little word changed the meaning from "he said" to "they said," and it made all the difference.

Within the year before he died, he bounded into the kitchen and said to my mom and me, "Guess what! I memorized the whole first chapter of Genesis. Do you want to hear? I memorized it in Hebrew." He was proud of himself. It wasn't enough to learn it in English; Dad was ecstatic to have learned it in Hebrew. I said yes to spare his feelings. As he was reciting, Mom started stretching. Then, she worked her way into cleaning up a little pile of something insignificant. He got to about verse 12 of Genesis Chapter 1 when he said, "Sara, you aren't listening to me so I'm going to stop." She said, "Reggie, I'm listening. I'm just trying to clean up a little bit."

He tried to say more, but my mom cleaning and not seeming to pay attention was really bothering him. He had always talked about wanting to memorize the whole Bible. The reason behind this wish was it was believed that Paul was in the Sanhedrin, an ancient Jewish council that was only made up of the brightest scholars of the Bible (made up only of the Old Testament at the time since the New Testament didn't exist), that he had to know all of the Old Testament by heart. Paul didn't have a Bible to take around every-where with him so Paul's writings and quotes from the Old Testament were memorized. The Holy Scriptures were written on scrolls, and it wasn't as if there were "pocket scrolls" or footnotes. And the scrolls of the Old Testament were kept in temples. Paul had to know the scriptures, the Old Testament, inside and out. He was always stating, "In the scriptures it says," and Dad wanted to do that. By the time Dad died, he had memorized the first four chapters of Genesis. First, he started to learn it in English, but as he began to learn Hebrew he changed to memorizing the chapters in Hebrew. Dad always thought Paul got a bad rap when English translations and leaders try to make him seem as if he was against the Old

Testament; and Dad wanted to be able to speak knowledgeably and quickly and precisely about such things. Paul was Jewish and knew all of the Old Testament, and he would not have contradicted what he had grown up learning. Memorizing the whole Bible, starting with Genesis 1 in Hebrew, would enable him to have knowledgeable, thorough discussions of the Bible at any time.

My dad was so interested in studying God, Hebrew, and the Bible, that my mom and I knew he would study until the day he died. If he died at 90 or 43 years old, he was going to find something new to study and learn. I hadn't seen my dad have this much passion for learning in all the years I had been alive. And while he admitted he never liked reading, when it came to God, his personal entertainment didn't matter. God became his entertainment. I was afraid that if he studied too much (he was already up to eight hours, seven days a week) he might actually question God's existence or Jesus being the Messiah. But, deep down, I knew he would never believe that. My dad was standing on a solid ground of faith. The question was just how far he wanted to be elevated toward learning about God and the truth and about His Word. He would never have said Jesus wasn't the Messiah or said that God didn't exist; he kept that constant throughout all his studying.

In August 2004, my dad stopped doing Bible studies. He didn't stop because he didn't believe in them, but because he didn't want to say incorrect things. He wanted to make sure everything he was saying was 100 percent true. He didn't want to be too extreme or not hard enough when he made certain points. My mom said if he wanted to get everything 100 percent he wouldn't be teaching for a long time because even the best don't get it right all of the time. Every once in a while, he would ask me questions to get me thinking about things I figure he was learning, but we never actually sat down and had another group Bible study after August.

One of those questions was, "Hey, Jeremy, what if I told you the Messiah was married and had a child? Would that surprise you?" I said, "Yeah, a little, because I didn't think he was married because of the New Testament we have. I don't see what's wrong with it, though, because it wasn't as if he was sinning." And he just looked at me and smiled. I know he was doing research on it, but he didn't want to give me any details until he was certain. I must admit I am interested to see his notes on that subject because I know he was writing it all down. I'm sure he would have had a field day with *The Da Vinci Code* film that was recently released. Yes, Jesus could have, but was he? I don't know yet.

There was one time when it was just my dad and me. I'll never forget. I was 18 years old, and I went into his office like I was interviewing for a job. We both had our Bibles open, and we started talking on the subject of God punishing someone for his sins. I told Dad that I didn't think God punished people directly, but that he set things up in the world to work out that if someone were to sin they would be punished for it. Similar to how he set up the laws of physics: if one jumps out of a building one will go down, not up. My dad said that he thought God punished us directly, and that He had everything to do with it. He used a verse from Isaiah about people believing that God was more than one person. In Isaiah 45: 6-7, God said (6) so all the world from east to west will know there is no other God. I am the LORD, and there is no other. (7) I am the one who creates the light and makes the darkness. I am the one who sends good times and bad times. I, the LORD, am the one who does these things.

Basically Dad said that God punishes people for doing wrong when a lot of people think it is Satan. That whole passage was talking about how there was no particular person who was "Satan" because *Satan* in Hebrew is not a pronoun. It is *hasatan* in Hebrew, and to ask anyone who knows Hebrew, "ha" before a word is the article *the*. Every time we read *Satan* in our Bibles we are really seeing, "the enemy" because that's what *Satan* means, "enemy, or adversary." We came to an agreement that God lets things happen to people and that he does things to certain people for disobeying. Basically we were both right. God intervenes at times, and at others, he lets things happen. But that was the first time I learned about a biblical passage that was clear that God was not fighting one specific enemy, but that Satan means "enemy" and is not just one being (To get into the reasoning behind every part of the Bible where Satan appears would take up too much space in this book. I can explain the snake in the garden, the story of Job, the story of Satan tempting God, just about anything. I still have to do my research on a few topics, but for the most part I can cover my bases.).

Dad never did anything halfway. He had fundamental differences in beliefs with Nehemia, who was teaching him Hebrew. During that time he kept saying, "I think I've found something, but I don't want to say anything yet. If I'm wrong, I don't want to alarm anybody." To hear him say he wanted to be 125 percent certain was something new. We appreciated that, too, because every time he found something new, he turned us on our heads. I did question whether or not he would ever share with us what he was learning because 100 percent certainty is a tall order. I would have loved to be able to sit down with him and to hear what his thoughts were on the subject he was studying. I look forward to reading over his notes and drawing my own conjectures. Maybe I could have helped him. Presently, all of his notes are packed in storage. I'm sure they are thorough; the only thing missing will be his enthusiasm. Soon we'll go through them. Together, when we're ready, we can share his last words. Another gift from Dad.

Epilogue

About two weeks after my father's death I went back to school. I walked into a campus coffee shop on a late January night, wearing my dad's Green Bay Packers jersey. After giving me my food, the manager looked up at me with his kind, wizened eyes and said, "Are you a Reggie White fan?"

"Yeah, I like him," I said. My heart beat a little faster.

"It's a shame what happened. That really caught me off guard. He was a heck of a man."

"Yeah, he was great." I couldn't say anymore.

He then asked me, "Do you know if his son came back to school? Is he doing all right?"

I held back a chuckle, smiled slightly, and said, "Yeah, he's back. He's doing fine."

"That's good," the guy said. "Well, you have a good night."

Outside, I told my roommate and some friends that story. Even after Dad's death, I still tried to hold on to my anonymity. I still wanted to be seen as a regular kid going into a coffee shop for some food. Much has changed throughout my life, but some things never will.

Before my dad died, I received a gift that many people never get. I always told myself that I'd win one of those contests I saw on Saturday morning cartoons that virtually no one I ever knew won. When I was younger, I told my mom that I would win a contest one day. But nearly all hope was lost when I wasn't "12 and under" anymore. But precisely around that age, things in my house started to change. I received an unparalleled knowledge of the Bible and what God wants me to do with my life. I learned the truth because of my father.

It is written that "You shall know the truth and the truth shall set you free." While I had known "the truth" for a long time, I never felt set free. Learning the truth about Christmas, Easter, dietary laws,

Hebrew traditions, Hebrew translation, Satan's real identity, and even hell, I realized, "I *am* set free." I felt peace. More specifically, I felt great that I was coming into a better relationship with the man who taught me everything I needed to grow up in this crazy place we call Earth.

When he died, I cried many hours, but I knew he would always be with me. I mourned mostly for what never was and never would be. Meeting my beautiful wife and giving his approval. Picking up his grandchildren and making the same jokes with them that he made with my sister and me. Going to the Super Bowl with him to watch the Eagles ultimately lose to the Patriots. Answering questions that only he can answer. Talking openly to him about my walk with God.

I will miss hearing his opinion on the Cowboys after they got T.O. I will miss being able to ask him, "Do you think Brett should play another year?" I will miss the man I saw him becoming and the man I was becoming because of him. I will miss him seeing my sister graduate from high school or seeing Mom being successful at her own real job in real estate. I will miss her coming home, telling him about her day at work. I will miss his phone calls, telling me the new things he learned about the Bible. I will miss the advice he was just beginning to give me as I got older that he didn't want to get into when I was younger. I will miss my father in the way a child that never had a father misses him.

As much as people like to see us differently, I the writer and my dad the football player, we are a lot alike. We both get sad at the same things. We both wear our hearts on our sleeves, and we both stand firm for what we believe. Both of us can debate someone into the ground. When people come up and ask me, "How was it growing up with Reggie White?" My response is this: "Reggie who? Oh, you mean my dad. He was my dad, that's all." Sure, when we'd go to Disney World people would take pictures without asking him and we'd get swamped by fans. Sure, it was annoying when a group of people surrounded him for autographs when we were just trying to go to the mall. Sure, it stunk when waiters and managers came to

I was very fortunate to have met several great professional athletes in my youth, such as the group shown here with my dad at the Pro Bowl.

the table to say, "I'd like to extend our welcome to you from this restaurant. By the way, can you sign this for me?" That was never something I enjoyed. But at the same time, I got a great father and a few perks. It was great going to football games, meeting my favorite players at the Pro Bowl, and being able to see as many U.S. and foreign cities as I did. But that stuff is not what was important.

He instilled in me a love and respect for God. If it hadn't been for my dad with all of his crazy ways, revelations of what he was doing right and wrong, and his silly attitude and ability to be a 41-year-old man who still watched cartoons, I would not be the man that I am today. But I understand why God would want my father close to Him.

Will my mom remarry? I don't know, but I hope so. I know that's what my dad would want, and I know she deserves it. She was always beside my dad even when she did not agree with him. She showed unwavering, unconditional love. I am proud of her because she is such a strong woman. I may have lost one parent, but I recognize all the people still around me. If she ever remarries, surely it will be tough to find someone who can fill my dad's shoes, literally and figuratively. But while it was God's will for my dad to go home, I know God will not forget my mom. As long as she's happy, I'm happy.

Yehovah is my father. He always has been and always will be. As I enter into my junior year of college, I know a few things because I've figured them out, but some, because my dad and mom raised me so well. Now I have to focus on what I need to do in my life, what The Father's will is for me in my life. I'll do what I always planned to do: get married, give my dad and my mom wonderful grandchildren, and find a job I enjoy. And as long as I know my dad is always with me, and I trust what he's taught me, I'll be okay. I am never alone. Despite strife, I am at peace, and I know not many people can say that. I know that when I get stressed or want to cry, it doesn't mean that I'm not at peace. I know that if I love God, I'll obey Him. And if I obey Him, my life will be exactly how my dad would have wanted. I can't think of anything better.

One quote my mom continues to harp on is, "Forgive, Live, Love, Laugh, and Pray." We all need to apply this to our lives to live fulfilling lives.

Acknowledgments

First, I would like to thank my mother for everything she's done for me. Mom, you've believed in me ever since I came out feet first. You told me I could do whatever I put my mind to, and you told me I should always be positive. That positive thinking has shaped me into the man I am today. I want to thank you for being the first one to tell me I should write this book when I decided to write it a week before dad's death.

I would like to thank my sister for being as wonderful as she is and for believing that I could write this book as well, even if she thinks it is too long to read.

I want to thank all of my teachers over the years from my nine schools. Some of those who have made the most impact were Mrs. Topi, Mrs. Chinn, Sister Philipia, Mrs. Clark, Mr. Nerness, Mr. Humphrey, and Mrs. Hallman. Thank you all for everything you have taught me about everything that was important to you.

To Amy Tyler, thank you so much for your hard work, edits, and revisions with this book, because without you, it wouldn't have been half of the book it is. Your tenacity and knowledge of both writing and me are priceless.

I want to thank Aunt Maria, Uncle Wayne, Wesley, Morgan, Shari Kiera, Uncle Steve, Grandmommy, and Granddaddy for always being there for me and realizing my "uniqueness," even when it seemed as if I was just odd.

I want to thank the city of Green Bay, Wisconsin; nothing against Philadelphia, but Green Bay will forever be my home, and I want to thank all of the people there, both whom I met and whom I didn't meet personally, for accepting the White family with open arms.

I want to particularly thank the Klarner family for being there for us when we first got to Green Bay for offering us sheets and pillows. You all would continue to be the greatest friends we

Here I am with my Aunt Janie, my Grandpa's oldest sister.

would ever have. You specifically made Green Bay worth being a part of.

I want to thank all my true friends over the years: the friends who are always able to look past the fact that I was the son of a superstar and accept me for me. I want to thank all those people who really became my close friends, who I can truly call my family, like Joe Pierre and Adam Klarner.

I want to thank everyone who ever taught my dad something about the Bible within the last four years of his life. What you all taught him will stay with me for the rest of my life.

Most of all, I want to thank Yehovah. The Father has given me so much strength to turn an idea into a reality. I want to thank Him for using me to deliver His message that He wants people to hear. I thank you, Lord, for helping me with this book; I know I needed it.

And lastly I want to thank my father. Although he is not physically here, he is with me and with everyone else he ever came into contact. And although we may not have always seen eye to eye, I thank God for what Dad taught me, because it helped shape me into the man I am today. Thank you so much, Dad, for everything you've given me, and I know I'll see you again one day. Until then, help me to become a wonderful husband like yourself, a great brother, son, and one day a great father to my children, who I will raise in the way of *The Father.*

Afterword

Finally, the weekend that I had been waiting to take part in all summer arrived. It was time to go to Canton, Ohio, for the NFL Pro Football Hall of Fame Inductions. As the event was steadily approaching, I was not ready for it to come, but I was kind of ready for it to be over. Don't get me wrong—I had been looking forward to the weekend of August 4 for seven months—but at the same time, I knew how emotionally taxing it would be on my family and me. Yes, it was an honor to have my dad recognized as one of the NFL's elite players, but it also meant that I would have to see him all over again. I would have to see his images online, in the newspapers, and most importantly, in the brass bust created in his honor. All I could do was hope for the best.

As the weekend approached, my mother suffered from a sudden onset of vertigo triggered by all of the stress she'd been dealing with this summer. She definitely had a lot on her plate: she was helping me with my book, getting my dad's commemorative DVD ready, and working as a realtor. Plus, she would be accepting my dad's award. I knew that after it was all over I would be able to rest, but it was even more reassuring to know that my mom would finally be able to take a break.

My mom's vertigo started to get better by August 3—a Thursday. She was late trying to get on her flight that morning, but that turned out to be a blessing in disguise. Missing her plane meant that she would get a chance to rest a little longer before starting what probably would be the biggest weekend that she would ever spend in honor of her husband. Needless to say, she was feeling much better when I took her to the airport later that afternoon.

Even though I was presenting the award to my mother, I did not go to Canton with her on that Thursday afternoon. I drove up with my family (Aunt Maria, Uncle Wayne, Wesley, Morgan, Kiera, and

Jecolia) the next day. And on the way to Ohio, I started videotaping the beginning of our memorable weekend.

When I got to Canton, I had to get ready immediately for a dinner in which the inductees would be presented with the honorary gold jacket. I didn't realize until that night that I would have to be everywhere my mom was for the rest of the weekend. For the next couple of days, we were attached at the hip because I was the presenter and she was accepting the award on my father's behalf.

When it was time for the NFL to present my dad with a jacket, my mom and I were presented with an honorary plaque. I know it doesn't sound like much, but it was a very unique plaque with the NFL patch logo on it along with a picture of my dad. It was classy and much better than the simple "high-school-making-the-grade-plaque" that I had envisioned. Before we went up on stage my mom said, "Jeremy, I've been walking around in these heels all day, and my feet are killing me. When we go up to receive the plaque you can go around the stage with it and show it to the audience while I stand in the middle and rest my feet a little bit."

I was extremely happy about this, since I've always wanted to redeem myself for not being able to run around the stadium during halftime in Green Bay, Wisconsin, when the Packers retired my dad's number. When I walked up on stage, I hoisted the plaque high in the air and walked around to the four corners of the stage. At the last corner, I pumped my fist in the air and showed the Super Bowl ring that my dad had gotten for me when we won Super Bowl XXXI. From then on, it would be funny to hear that a lot of people thought that it was my dad's ring. I told them my dad's ring was almost twice as large.

On Saturday morning, I woke up at the atrocious hour of 5:45 a.m. to take part in a parade. When we arrived, there were so many floats and bands that I felt like I could have been in New York City. Thousands of people lined up along the street ready to see the Hall of Fame inductees and their presenters. I enjoyed this part of the trip very much, but there was an awkward moment, and it was not caused by me. When my mom and I passed the people along the

Here I'm raising the honorary plaque presented to us by the Hall of Fame.

sides of the street they would clap, whistle and scream, "Reggie! Reggie! We miss you, Reggie! Go, Reggie! Yeah, Reggie! Thanks, Reggie!"

People were very excited to see my mom and me. Sadly, many of them did not know that I was not my dad. For instance: we passed one lady, and she tried to get a picture of us while we were rolling past her in the convertible we were in. She said, "Reggie!" I looked back and waved because I figured she thought maybe I was Reggie White Jr. or that she was just trying to acknowledge my dad. But then she saw my name on the side of the car and called, "Jeremy?"

"Yes?"

"Are you Reggie's son?"

"Yeah!"

Then she shouted, "WHERE'S YO DADDY?"

My mom heard this and immediately we just looked at each other and kind of laughed. We turned around and didn't respond. The crowd around her sat hushed in amazement. My mother and I assumed that someone would tell her, and I'm sure that, when she found out, she felt pretty bad. She would either bad for saying it or stupid for not knowing. It baffled me, but I finally felt more of a connection with my mom when she told me that people still send her items in the mail to be signed by my dad. I would have thought that you had to have been living under a rock to not know that my dad had passed away.

As the day progressed, it was time for inductions, and it was getting closer to the time for my speech to introduce my dad and mom. At the back of the stage, I remember talking to Dan Marino, Steve Young, Lawrence Taylor, and other Hall of Fame inductees. I was amazed that I, Jeremy White, was having a conversation with these guys and that they were treating me as if they had seen my dad again. Most of the people who knew my dad would look at me in astonishment because they either couldn't believe how much I had grown, or they were amazed by how much I resemble my father.

It was amusing when my sister sang the national anthem because the NFL told her to start without introducing her. Everyone in the audience was still talking, walking around, and going about their business when, all of a sudden, the sweetest voice started to sing, "O say can you see ..." and a hush fell over the crowd instantly. As she finished I was very proud of her because she did a great job, but it was time to focus on what I needed to do. I wanted to do well because this day was all about my dad.

As other people spoke before me, I started to get more and more comfortable with my speech. This was not because of arrogance, but because I knew that what I was about to say would touch people in a way that God and my dad would have wanted people to be touched. As I walked up to the podium, I felt as if I might break down right then. This was entirely unexpected because I didn't think I would cry before the speech—maybe during or after, but not before. But I continued, and as I was finishing up my speech, I felt a sense of pride that I hadn't felt in a while. I knew my dad was proud of me and that the great things I said about him as a person were true.

I was extremely excited to unveil the bust for the whole world to see. As my mom and I pulled back the cloth that covered my father's image, I was smiling. As the cloth came off, I stole one look at the bust and started to say, "It doesn't look like him, does it?" Suddenly, I noticed my mom's face starting to purse as if she were about to begin crying. Then my face did the same. I looked again at the bust and realized it was an exact replica of my dad, and that's when I lost it. It was as if I were seeing him again. It wasn't just a picture, it was his entire head in 3D, and for a minute, I felt like I was looking at my dad's compassionate face again, knowing the sad truth that it was not him. The bronze bust did not possess his spirit. Even though John Madden mentioned that he believes the busts talk to each other at night when everyone is gone, I knew my dad would not be saying, "Hey, Son, you did a good job," to me right then. The bust was not him; but it sure looked like him, and it hurt. It hurt so bad that I broke down and couldn't stop sobbing during most of my mom's acceptance speech.

After the ceremony, I took pictures with the bust and one of the craziest things happened. Roger Staubach came and introduced himself to me. I have been a Dallas Cowboys fan since I was four years old, and the quarterback who led them to the Super Bowl in the 1970s came and introduced himself to me. I had been trying to get a glimpse of him all weekend, but he found me. That seemed backward to me. He told me that I did a great job, but while he was talking, I couldn't stop thinking, "You are a legend. You played for the Dallas Cowboys. You are Roger Staubach here shaking my hand! COOL!"

The day was not over. After the induction ceremony was finished, I went to a trailer occupied by the NFL Network. They interviewed my mom and me with Steve Mariucci. And then I saw (NFL Network lead anchor) Rich Eisen. As he came up to me, he said, "Hi, Jeremy, I'm Rich Eisen!" I said, "Hello, Mr. Eisen, thank you for

I spoke with one of my favorite Dallas Cowboys quarterbacks, Roger Staubach. Although I'd met him before, he initiated this conversation, which I appreciated.

having us." He said, "Call me Rich." I couldn't believe that Rich Eisen was telling me to call him "Rich." I don't know if I'll ever be able to refer to anyone six or seven years older than I am by their first name.

The next morning, I went to a lunch that was called the "Roundtable." At this function, the Hall of Fame brought all the inductees up on stage to talk about their experiences. I remember them talking a lot about my dad. John Madden almost cried when he was talking about how great a player and person my dad was, and my mom starting crying yet again. Talk about a rough three days. It was funny, though, when Mr. Madden said he was wearing his 'give-up' shoes. He had been walking around so much that he didn't care what his shoes looked like as long as they were comfortable. My mom said she was also wearing her 'give-ups' or more commonly known as non-high-heeled shoes.

Mr. Madden made it a point to say, "Well Sara, at least your give-ups look better than mine."

The Hall of Fame weekend felt a lot like my dad's funeral. Many people came up to me and said, "Your dad was a great man; he gave me so much hope as a believer." Or they would say, "He was a great player; my dad died too, so I know what you are going through." Or I would hear, "Your dad was one of a kind, I know he'd be so proud of you right now."

People had so many positive things to say about him. So many people were using the word 'bittersweet' to describe the weekend my family and I were having. Yes, it hurt, but it was not bitter. I was not bitter against God for taking him. I know my dad was taken for a reason, and I am realizing that reason more and more every day. It makes perfect sense to me. He was ready to go, and God found the perfect time to take him. I don't disagree with God's will, and just because it involved my dad dying, I am not disagreeing with it now. It was a sweet time, it really was. What the NFL was doing for my dad was wonderful. It was sweet that the media embraced him. It was sweet that so many people were still praying for our family even after a year and a half.

Some might call this an ending. I can't honestly tell you that there will ever be an ending. My dad, Reggie White, will live on forever in our memories. I am honored to consider the Hall of Fame weekend a memorable one, and yes, sweet.

Jeremy White
August 2006